Walks
in
Wester Ross

by

Mary Welsh

Maps and illustrations by
David Macaulay

Westmorland Gazette, Kendal, Cumbria.

First published 1991

ISBN 0 902272 86 1

Published by
Westmorland Gazette
22 Stricklandgate, Kendal, Cumbria

Printed by
Dixon Printing Co. Ltd.
Burneside Road, Kendal, Cumbria.

Walks
in
Wester Ross

Preface

Wester Ross, a startlingly dramatic and hauntingly beautiful area of mountains, rocky moorland, golden sands and abundant plant and wildlife, lies in the north west of Scotland. Its shores, warmed by the Gulf Stream, can support palm trees and exotic vegetation where suitably protected from the westerlies. Inland, many of Scotland's Munros (mountains over 3000 feet) are found, rearing upwards, jagged and menacing, a great attraction for all climbers and hill walkers.

This lovely area stretches from Lochcarron in the south to the River Kirkaig in the north. Fingers of the Inner Sound of Raasay and The Minch create the tranquil sea lochs of Carron, Kishorn, Torridon, Gairloch, Little Loch Broom and Loch Broom. Inland lochs, large and small, lie round the corner on nearly every walk. Loch Maree, perhaps the jewel in the crown, is closely followed by Fionn Loch, Lochan Fada and Loch na Sealga in my rating of peacefulness, solitude and range of colours.

The opportunity to get away into the hills or along the seashore has brought me back time and again to this lovely corner of Scotland. It is a rare pleasure in these noisy days to walk where the only sounds are those of bees seeking nectar from the heather; the wind tangling in lonely corries or among the highest branches of trees; the haunting calls of the eagle, the oyster-catcher or meadow pipit; and the crashing of the sea about the rocks.

In this book, I have included walks into forests, beside tumbling burns, to remote inland lochs, along cliff tops, to ruined villages, to sites of ancient relics, across a carpet of moorland where rocky outcrops push through, over hill passes and up high mountains. I have tried to write something for all tastes. The shortest walk is half a mile and the longest 11 miles.

Look for the location of each walk in the area map at the front of the book. For a rough guide, use the small maps accompanying each walk, but always supplement these by using the relevant Ordnance Survey maps. I have used the O.S. 1:50,000 Landranger Series maps, and the appropriate sheet numbers for each walk are given on the contents page. On these the footpaths, marked in black dashed lines, and the tracks, in double dashed lines, are as definite and reliable as the maps imply.

For each walk I have given the plants, birds, insects and views I have seen and hope this will help you to see some of the same. Wester Ross is a wonderful area, but to seek out the solitude of this vast, rugged, remote district requires leaving the car and walking. For most of the walks, walking boots are essential. It does rain and therefore good waterproofs need to be carried. Always take extra food, including some high-energy food. Carry a compass — and know how to use it — a whistle, a torch, a small first-aid kit, a survival bag and spare clothing. Generally these items are not needed but one day they might.

One of the most attractive sights is of a herd of deer moving across the side of a mountain corrie. The deer are an important crop in the economy of the region. From mid-August onwards, when shooting may be taking place, check locally if you intend to cross the moors.

I cannot end this preface without mentioning those members of my family, Tom, Edward, John and Sarah, and my friend Joan Morgan, who walked with me and tested all the routes described. I am extremely grateful for their patience and endurance when a route had to be retraced to get it absolutely correct or when they allowed me to remain stationary for a long time to watch the abundant wildlife. I must also record my grateful thanks to David Macaulay, who has once again illustrated a book of walks for me with unerring accuracy and sympathetic style.

Good walking!

Map of Wester Ross

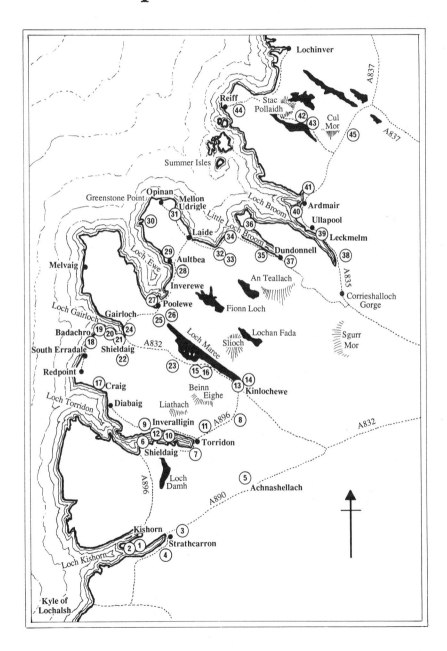

Contents

Contents (continued)

1. A Circular Walk from Strome Castle via Ardaneaskan and the Forest

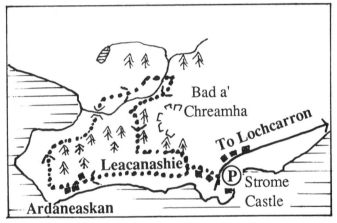

O.S. reference 863355

The village of Lochcarron, formerly called Jeantown, is composed of greystone cottages that stretch along the lochside. Drive south west from the village and turn left, then travel for three miles along the lochshore road. Just beyond the right turn for Ardaneaskan, park on the grass verge on the left between derelict buildings, opposite the ruins of Strome Castle. Walk to the jetty at the end of the road where the North Strome to South Strome ferry once plied. Much of the traffic from the north for the Isle of Skye used the ferry and long queues of traffic built up. Now all is peaceful because the main road to Skye runs on a road built on the far side of the loch.

Return along the road and take the gated footpath up to the courtyard of Strome Castle. Built in the 15th century, and demolished after a siege in 1602, it was originally part of the lands of the ancient earldom of Ross. In 1472 Celestine, son of Alexander Earl of Ross, gave the castle to Alan Cameron of Lochiel. The charter was confirmed by James IV in 1495 but in 1539 it was revoked by James V and the castle given to the Macdonalds of Glengarry.

From that time there was continual struggle for possession of the castle between the Macdonalds and their neighbours, the Mackenzies of Kintail. In 1602, Mackenzie of Kintail laid siege to the castle. He was about to admit failure when women from the castle went out to draw water from the well. On their return, frightened and in a poor light, they poured the water into a vat containing gunpowder. When the defenders came to replenish their stock they discovered what had happened. A Mackenzie prisoner in the castle heard the Macdonalds cursing the women. He escaped and told his chief who immediately renewed the attack. The Macdonalds sued for peace, and were allowed to leave safely, whereupon the Mackenzies blew up the castle and it has remained a ruin ever since.

Climb through the arch in the seaward wall and look out over the loch to the magnificent peaks on Skye. Small boats lie anchored in the bay, sandpipers fly quickly along the shore and herring gulls call raucously.

Walk back to the signposted road to Ardaneaskan and begin the steady climb upwards. In wet areas grow juncus, spearwort, butterwort, flags and cotton grass. In drier parts flower tormentil, heather and eyebright. Here a pair of redstarts raise their brood. Follow the road below outcrops of rock and then downhill, past a small bay where dog-rose is laden with deep pink blossoms. Continue onwards past a huge overhang where wood sage grows, and primroses flower in spring. Walk past the dwellings at Leacanashie.

The road climbs steadily beneath deciduous trees, and through gaps can be seen glorious views of the loch and the magnificent mountains over the water. Walk through a tunnel of

coniferous trees and stride on past the small settlement of Ardaneaskan. Sit on the wooden bench on a knoll beyond the end of the metalled road and savour the view. Plockton lies across the water, its houses brilliantly white in the bright sunlight.

Return to the road end and walk north along the rough access road. This crosses open moorland, with grand views ahead of tree-covered towering crags. Look down on Loch Reraig to the left, where oyster-catchers call noisily and a heron waits patiently for prey.

Cross the bridge over the Reraig Burn. To the left lies Reraig Cottage. Continue through two gates into the forest. Walk along the delightful path close by the burn. It is bordered with alders. Where the path divides, take the right fork. This soon leads to an open area with the craggy north side of Bad a' Chreamha towering over all. Follow the forest road, where dragonflies flit, as it drops downhill beside the burn once more.

Walk across the concrete bridge over the burn and turn right along the forest road. This gradually climbs high above the burn and there are more views of Skye over the tree tops. Look for a narrow path off left where the forest road makes a sharp turn to the left. The waymark — a red arrow on a white background — has been moved a short way along the path while work to extract timber has been in progress. Beyond the waymark, the narrow path is a joy to walk. it climbs steadily through the trees skirting the western slopes of Bad a' Chreamha. Look for evidence of pine marten — dark coiled droppings on stones along the path.

Follow the path where it begins to descend through dense conifers, until it joins a forest road. Turn left and walk the short distance to the end. Here move to the right and take the narrow track left that descends through deciduous trees and ferns, where foxgloves stand tall. Follow this delightful path downhill until it joins the road at Leacanashie. Turn left and walk back to Strome Castle.

5 miles
3 hours

2. Circular Walk to Achintraid from Leacanashie on Loch Carron

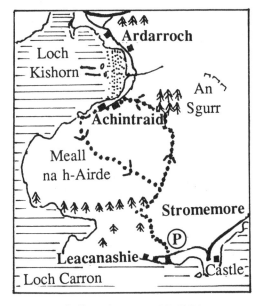

O.S. reference 856351

Leave Lochcarron as for Walk 1 and park off the road at Leacanashie, in a cleared area on the right. The footpath, indistinct at first, rapidly becomes clearer as it ascends the hillside, where many trees have been felled. Follow it as it moves into the trees, passing beneath huge, shading cypresses onto a forest road. Turn left and then after 20 yards take a clearly-waymarked path leading off right.

Stride along this as it ascends steadily into the forest. The call of hungry young peregrines echoes eerily over the conifers. Follow the path as it drops downhill to the valley of the Reraig Burn. Turn right where the path joins a forest road and walk as far as the bridge over the burn. Do not cross but continue for 30 yards to a cairned path going off left. Look for dog lichen growing at the side of the way.

Cross the Reraig Burn and climb steadily beneath the tall coniferous trees that crowd the path. On either side of the path, about the forest floor, lie huge boulders, heavily encrusted with moss and lichen. Towards the end of the path, before the forest gate, it becomes treacherously wet. Tread carefully here, perhaps moving into the trees, to find a reasonably dry way.

Beyond the gate, walk on along the good path beneath birch. Cross the Reraig where it is cairned on either bank; there is a small causeway of stones to help you across. Walk on to the open moorland — Blar nan Clachan Mora — following a good path passing through a heather garden and keeping close to the Reraig. Look for young trout darting downstream in the burn.

Walk along the well-cairned path as it climbs away from the burn below the southern slopes of An Sgurr. On reaching a cairn, which sits high on an ancient wall covered with heather and bracken, turn left. Step out along a wide track. Look left across the moorland to pleasing views of the forest and the mountains beyond. Continue ascending the cairned track until the brow is reached. Lovely Loch Kishorn lies below — a blue, blue bay with sandy beaches. Small white cottages lie scattered round the bay and behind these lie more mixed plantings. Beyond lies the Bealach na Bà — the pass of cattle — an old drove road. Today a motor road surmounts the pass with much winding and curving as it passes between high mountains on either side.

Follow the track as it bears to the right. At the forest fence, the path turns left and drops steadily downhill. Stonechats call from the tops of bracken stalks. Pass through the gate and walk down a tree-lined track to the shore road. Turn left and walk past the dwellings of Achintraid, steadily climbing. Pass through the gate and walk down a tree-lined track to the shore road. Turn left and walk past the dwellings of Achintraid, steadily climbing. Pass through the gate and walk on along the metalled road.

Just beyond the road end, the way continues as an unmade access road into the forest. Turn left up the hillside just before the gate into the plantation. A high wire deer fence climbs uphill. Keep in sight of this for the return walk over the moorland. After passing through silver birch woodland, you reach the higher moors. There is a path of sorts in some places but generally the going is wet and the ground full of tussocks.

Pass Lochan Dubha and enjoy its reeded margins and large patches of white water lilies. A brood of stonechats sits on the deer fence, causing consternation to the parents, who flit around calling in a distressed manner. From here, strike over to the left to avoid a small lochan and much very wet ground around it. Then begin the descent, following the deer fence to the plantation. Follow the fence to the left, crossing the winding feeder streams of the Reraig until the gate into the forest is regained.

From here, return by the same route used at the outset of this glorious seven-mile tramp.

7 miles
4 hours

14

3. A Walk around Maol Chean-dearg, Lochcarron

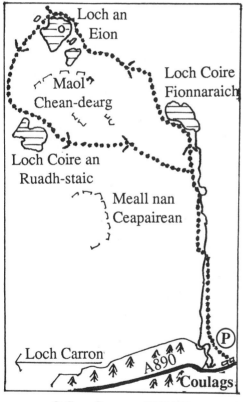

O.S. reference 957451

This is an 11-mile walk that could take six to eight hours. Its paths are well defined but it includes much hill walking and should be attempted only by strong walkers. On a fine day the views are breathtaking. Avoid this route during September and October when deer stalking is in progress.

Park in the wide gravelly area beyond Coulags Bridge, on the right if coming from Lochcarron. Cross the road and follow a driveway towards a large bungalow. Move left at a fence boundary, following a footpath sign. The path takes you through deciduous

woodland close to the Fionn-abhainn burn. Beyond the trees, the small path is lined with heather, cotton grass and bog asphodel, orchid and round-leaved sundew. It joins the track that climbs gently through the glen, with glorious views ahead. Overhead a merlin flies low, twisting sharply in flight as it hunts.

Pass through a rusty gate in a rusty wire fence that stretches across the glen. Continue ascending, as quartzite-topped cones of mountains come into view. Follow the path as it comes to the edge of the burn and cross by the footbridge. Turn right and head along the clear path deeper into the glen.

The path, rough in places and wet after rain, is most distinct. It is bordered with the aromatic bog myrtle and bonsai willows and birches. It passes through a heather garden before reaching an old house, shaded by a gnarled rowan. This has been restored by the bothy association to provide a shelter for walkers.

Follow the path as it continues close to the left-hand bank of the burn, where another rowan grows. As the path moves away from the hurrying water, look right to a standing stone, Clach nan Con-fionn — a stone to which the legendary Fionn tethered his dogs!

At the cairned fork in the path, continue straight ahead, steadily climbing towards the head of the glen. And then Loch Coire Fionnaraich lies below, with two pairs of sandpipers busily flitting about the pebbly margins of the still water. A dipper feeds at the far side.

Pause by the loch and enjoy the intense peace before beginning the steady climb ahead. Look for frogs in damp areas and for the oblong-leaved sundew. At the cairn, turn left to continue ascending the pass of Bealach na Lice, shadowed occasionally by the Munro, Maol Chean-dearg. Look for alpine lady's mantle, now in seed, and for two species of bearberry.

Once you are over the top of the pass, several small lochans lie below and the glorious Loch an Eion, all cradled by rocky slopes. Golden rod grows scattered between the large boulders, white lousewort thrives on the heather roots and procumbent juniper flourishes. A dozen grouse fly up noisily and head towards quieter slopes. Towards Torridon lie the slopes of Beinn Alligin, with the route up via Tom na Gruagaich clearly visible.

Continue around the edge of the loch, with its small islands, to the cairn. From here, look north to see the jagged top of Liathach. Ahead, north-west, lies Beinn Damh. At the cairn, turn left and begin the steady climb away from the loch with one last look at a pair of divers on the still waters. Once you are over the brow, a grand view of Loch Carron and the mountains of Skye lies ahead.

Follow the path as it contours around the steep slopes of Maol Chean-dearg, where red deer feed high up on patchy grass. To the right in a hollow, lies Loch Coire an Ruadh-staic, reflecting the terraced barrenness of An Ruadh-stac beyond. The path continues climbing into this lunar landscape through a delightful floral garden. After further steady climbing along the clear path, look right to two more lovely lochans set in a quartzite bowl. Here droppings of deer and grouse abound, and deer hoofprints are much in evidence.

At this point, the path continues to the top of the ridge, but do not follow it. Strike up left instead to the pass between the south ridge of Maol Chean-dearg and Meall nan Ceapairean. The clear white path is soon attained and then the long descent to the glen begins. It zig-zags continually, reducing the gradient, until you reach the cairn passed much earlier on the walk. To the right lies the standing stone and a glimpse of the chimney pots of the bothy. Turn right and begin the long tramp back through the glen.

Avoid this route during the September to October stalking season.

11 miles
6-8 hours

4. Circular Walk from Achintee, Strathcarron

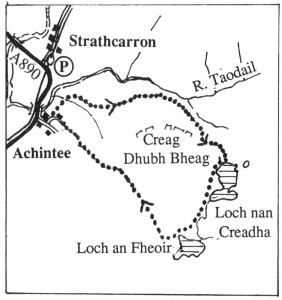

O.S. reference 942421

Park in the yard of Strathcarron Station. Walk along the A890 westwards. Look across the River Taodail to a row of holes high up on a sandstone cliff above the hurrying water. Watch the parent sand martins fly in and out, trying to satisfy their clamorous young. Take the signposted left turn to the village of Achintee, one-fifth of a mile along. Cross the cattle-grid and

walk uphill. Bear left and then right, passing sheep pens on the left and an electricity sub-station on the right.

Continue along the very rough road and turn left, walking over an indistinct moorland path just above the fence. Follow the cairned way over the low slopes to the side of a small burn, the Allt an-t Sagairt. Cross on convenient boulders, then pass a cairn, walking uphill on a clear, rough path. Look carefully into the steep gorge on the right, which is lined with rowan and birch.

To the left is a good view of the south shoulder of Maol Chean-dearg and the summit beyond (see Walk 3). An Ruadh-stac stands sparkling white to the left of the Munro. The path comes close to the Taodail burn and within sound of its racing water. Pass through the gateposts of an old fence and continue to the side of a tributary burn that flows out of Loch nan Creadha far above, and one of the targets of this walk. Look at the pretty falls below the ford over the burn, where a dipper feeds.

Do not cross the ford but begin the long, steady climb to the right. Enjoy the grand waterfall that tumbles through ferns, heather and birch in a series of sparkling jets. It rages down huge steps in the gorge. Walk on through the moorland below Creag Dhubh Bheag, remaining on the right side of the burn. Do not attempt to cross its deeply-cut meanderings — but if it is almost dry, look for the remains of ancient tree roots deep in the peat and exposed by the hurrying water in times of heavy rainfall. Walk on until the side of the delightful Loch nan Creadha is attained.

Here a decision has to be made — whether to turn back and retrace the outward way or, if the weather is good and you enjoy

a boggy, rough, pathless, exhilarating moorland walk, to continue. If the latter, turn right and walk along the side of the pretty, reeded loch keeping well up the slope. Stride on, without losing height, parallel with a feeder stream flowing from Loch an Fheòir, the loch that lies ahead. Continue beside the second loch, crossing a small tributary, to the clear path ahead. Turn right and begin the long descent. Along the path and about the little stream and lochshore are hoofprints left by deer, but of the animals there is no sign. Grouse fly up noisily, leaving the young heather shoots on which they have been feeding.

Enjoy the good views of Strathcarron, backed by wild mountain slopes, as you descend to Achintee.

5 miles
3-4 hours

5. Circular Walk from Achnashellach via Coulin Pass, Easan Dorcha and the River Lair

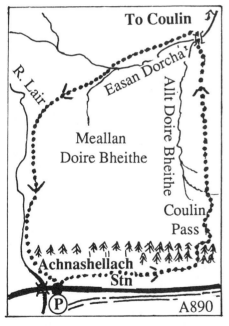

O.S. reference 004485

Park by the phone box or in the large space near the entrance to the lane to Achnashellach Station on the A890, eight miles from Lochcarron. Walk up the lane through rhododendrons, sycamore, birch, alder and oak to the station. Cross the line with care and walk into Achnashellach Forest. At a junction of several paths, avoid the left and right turn and walk straight ahead. Stride up the steadily climbing forest road through a variety of conifers full of goldcrests and coal tits.

Cross the dilapidated forest bridge over a deep gorge and enjoy the racing fall to the left. Look through a gap in the trees for a grand view to Glen Carron, far below. Overhead wings a young buzzard. Black coiled droppings left along the ride remind the walker of the elusive, generally nocturnal, pine marten.

Continue climbing the gently graded road. Watch for red deer feeding on the grass below the conifers and walk on to the forest gate. Beyond lies the Coulin Pass. Step out along the rough road, with heather moorland on either side, where orchis and bog asphodel flower. Pass a radio antenna and a rain gauge on the right side. Enjoy the magnificent views ahead of the quartzite top of Beinn Eighe and the mass of Slioch. Below, Loch Coulin comes into view.

Just before you reach the bridge over the Easan Dorcha, a large area of natural Scots pine begins. Turn left at the bridge and walk upstream along a rough track, keeping a dark plantation of firs to the right. Look for the delightful waterfall in the gorge to the left, descending white-topped under the pine and silver birch.

Walk on beside the tumbling burn where huge hardheads bloom. Notice the extensive area of natural pines stretching up the steep slopes opposite. Just before the bridge, a small bothy provides shelter if the weather turns inclement. Cross the bridge and look up to the magnificent waterfalls, overshadowed by birch and a huge Scots pine. About the banks grow heather, bracken and bilberry. A grey wagtail flies upstream and stonechats scold from a nearby fence.

Continue along the clear, narrow path as it winds uphill beside the waterfall. Follow it as it starts to cross an extensive basin of moorland, littered with boulders. Soon the Scots pine are left behind and the moorland path crosses the lower eastern skirts of Beinn Liath Mhór.

Gradually the path climbs out of the boulder field. Look for tadpoles and newts in a moorland pool. To the right lies the path winding up towards Bealach Bàn and Bealach na Lice. Bearberry is now in fruit and alpine lady's mantle is in seed. Club moss grows sparsely on this high ground.

Follow the cairned path, ignoring both right forks, until far below Loch Dùghaill comes into sight. The old stalkers' path now drops unrelentingly, boulder-strewn but clear, with Fuar Tholl to the right. Just before the forest is reached, two short paths turn off right to the bank of the River Lair. The first leads to a precarious viewpoint for the dramatic waterfalls racing down a drop in the tree-lined deep gorge below. The second comes to a deep pool below some magnificent cascades.

Walk into the forest. Just beyond two large gateposts (no gate), walk 50 paces ahead to come to a row of white stones set across the path. Here turn left, just before a feeder stream, to pick up the forest track. Turn right and stride out along the level forest track, looking back regularly to see splendid views of Fuar Tholl (known as Wellington's nose), towering above the tall conifers. At the three-way forest-track junction, turn right and walk down to the station.

Mid-August to the end of October is the deer stalking season. Arrange access with the estate office.

8 miles
6 hours

6. Circular Walk around the Headland North of Shieldaig

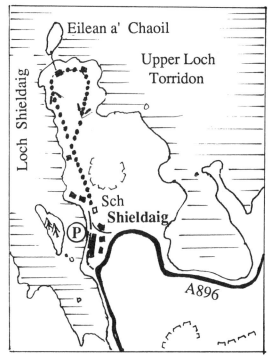

O.S. reference 815545

Park on the shore in front of the cottages at Shieldaig (Norse for herring bay). Walk north past the delightful ribbon of dwellings. From the beach comes the constant piping of noisy oyster-catchers. Across the still waters of Loch Shieldaig lies the wooded Shieldaig Island. Climb uphill and walk along the rough road in front of the primary school. Turn left at the junction and follow the rough track. Where the road forks, bear to the right and continue along it as it swings left.

The path runs along low cliffs, overlooking Loch Shieldaig, through heather, bracken, willow and silver birch. Overhead flies a merlin. Ahead are grand views of indentations in the rocky coastline and, beyond, lies the Inner Sound.

The good, distinct path drops down, passing between ferns and beneath birch. Just beyond the trees, a small path leads off left down the slopes to a pebbly sheltered beach. Continue along the main path as it climbs to a greensward from where you can look into the bay, with its several ruined crofts, and over the loch to the Applecross peninsula.

Stroll on along the delightful path past more inlets. Look right for a view of Inveralligin with Beinn Alligin behind and the peak of Liathach in the distance. Where the path forks and is cairned, turn left. Follow cairns up a huge lump of Torridonian sandstone to the clear path above. The path becomes a little rougher as it moves in from the cliff edge and then drops down a slope to a grassy way across a flat area.

The delightful path now moves towards the cliff edge again; look down on people fishing from a small boat just off another pebbly beach. To the side of the bay grows a huge aspen, its leaves quivering noisily in the sea breeze.

Walk on and then divert to the left from the path to sit on the promontory overlooking Loch Torridon. Several shags fly overhead and then return, travelling just above the surface of the water. Look back up Loch Shieldaig to the cottages of the village nestling round the bay.

Return to the path and follow it as it drops down to the shore. If the tide is out, climb over the rocks and clamber to the top of Eilean a' Chaoil. To the right lies the village of Torridon at the head of Upper Loch Torridon.

Leave the island and walk back along the path. Turn left onto a narrow path that passes between a solitary dwelling and its two wooden sheds. Follow it up the slope, clambering over an outcrop of rock, to a flat area above. Continue on the indistinct path to a small clump of birches. Pass through these and then cross over the intervening pasture to another dwelling. Turn right here and walk uphill (south) to pick up a good path that passes over a causeway, which crosses a large marshy area to the right. Ravens fly overhead, settling on a flat boulder high above.

Where the path becomes indistinct because of rocky outcrops, continue ahead, keeping the fish farm to your left. And then the path becomes distinct again. It passes through a clump of birch and then keeps to the edge of the trees until reaching the cairn, where the path divided earlier.

From here, return along the path taken on the approach route. This is a glorious cliff-top walk on a fine day. But remember the children who, in days gone by, had to take this route in all kinds of weather to walk to school from the croft houses on the headland. Remember, too, the postman.

3 miles
2 hours

7. Torridon (Annat) to Beinn Damh Return

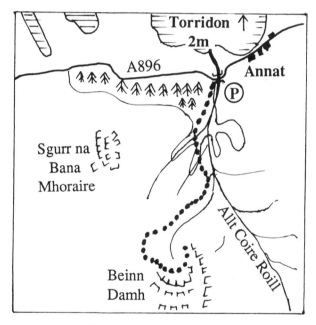

O.S. reference 888541

Head west from Annat on the A896 and park on the grass verge at the left-hand side of the road, close to the bridge over the Allt Coire Roill. Walk 20 yards to a tiny path leading left through some huge, overhanging rhododendrons to a small gate. This path is very easy to miss. Beyond the gate the wide, gently

ascending path rises through Scots pine and larch. Tiny rowans grow on the forest floor.

The path continues along the edge of a ravine through which the burn tumbles tempestuously on its journey to Upper Loch Torridon. Bilberry and male fern with fertile and infertile fronds thrive between the lofty pines. On a boulder in the path a fox has left its characteristic droppings.

The morning sun slants through the trees and from the branches come the chatterings of long-tailed tits. Some of these small birds chase each other through the twigs and others search the pine needles for insects. The sun catches the silvery threads of a myriad of tiny webs slung by small spiders between the needles and the branch. A ringlet dragonfly flits over the path, its body longer than that of the tits. Goldcrests seeking prey in the bark of the branches call quietly to each other. A wood wasp buzzes loudly as it flies between the trunks of the pines.

Cross the tributary stream by the causeway and follow the path as it moves away from the river through the trees. Keep to it as it swings to the right, continuing its upward climb and then returning once more to the side of the ravine. The river lies far below. Find a gap in the birches that line the edge of the canyon for a good view of the magnificent waterfall, where the Roill descends from the higher slopes. The noise of the falling water fills the air.

As the forest ends, the path divides. The right fork is the way to take for the mountain tops ahead. The path, easy to walk for most of the way, continues over the moorland, now a blaze of colour. Heather, tormentil, cotton grass and orchis — pink and

white — star the pastures. A small frog hops over the sphagnum and meadow pipits flit from rock to rock piping plaintively.

Continue along the path, looking back often to the ever-extending views. Small white cottages hug the shore of the loch and Liathach, with its seven peaks, towers grandly above. From here, you can see Beinn Alligin and the route to the summit of Beinn Damh. Beinn Eighe stretches away in the distance and Beinn Dearg sits between Alligin and Liathach.

The path comes close to Allt an Tuill Bhain, which issues from the coire above. Look for alpine lady's mantle, covered in pale lemon flowers, growing about the path. Sundew, thyme, milkwort, bedstraw and eyebright thrive along the way. Among the bilberry covering the slopes flower hawkweed, scabious, lousewort and golden rod. Follow the cairns as the path becomes less distinct. Look left into the coire, Toll Ban, a mass of rock and grassy patches.

Mossy saxifrage, covered with delicate white flowers, thrives on mats of sphagnum about the path, which leads onto the saddle. From here there are magnificent views of Loch Damh and Beinn Shieldaig beyond. To the south lies mountain after mountain with bright blue lochans between. Turn left and follow the clear, narrow path up the rocky slopes. This is another easy climb coming close to the cliff edge for a short way. Stag's horn club moss and fir club moss grow here and Iceland moss (a lichen) flourishes. Short-stemmed golden rod covered with bright yellow flowers brightens the way.

Follow the cairns as you ascend and continue along the faint path over a flatter area. Immediately ahead lies the cone shaped summit, its sides a mass of shattered quartzite boulders. Look for the line of cairns leading straight up over the tumbled boulders. This is not as arduous as it seems at first because the rough surface of the rocks gives a good grip to your boots. Notice the tiny patches of moss where grouse have fed on the vegetation and left their cylindrical droppings.

On the summit plateau thin grass grows and there are fewer boulders. A shelter lies to the left. Make use of the protection it gives you from the wind to enjoy the magnificent view.

From this summit the walker can walk over the more arduous route to the second summit. Or if you have climbed enough, return the same way. Do not forget to follow the cairns over the flatter area below the quartzite-covered summit and then continue along the full length of the saddle. Look for the cairn denoting the path down, just below the skirts of Meall Gorm.

5 miles
5 hours

8. Walk beside Loch Clair and Loch Coulin

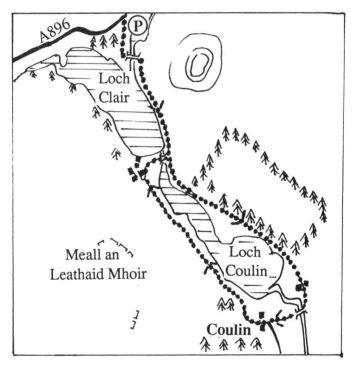

O.S. reference 001581

Park in either of two lay-bys on the Torridon to Kinlochewe road, close to the metalled lane leading to Coulin Lodge. (Do not park in the nearest passing place as this obstructs the easy flow of traffic).

The lane to Coulin Lodge leads down to a bridge over the river that leaves Loch Clair. To the right, a young plantation of birch and conifers stretches away to the slopes of Sgurr Dubh. A tiny newt sets off to wetter pastures on the other side of the road where bog myrtle, heather, scabious and eyebright cover the moorland. In the small lochan to the left of the bridge fishermen cast their lines.

Beyond the bridge, the road continues well above the waters of Loch Clair. After some 250 yards birch, alder and ferns clothe the steep banks. On the loch a black-throated diver idles in the sunshine and when it does dive it stays under for what seems a very long time.

Walk on beside the loch to the end of the road and then continue along the semi-reinforced track, as directed by the signpost. To the right lies the burn connecting Loch Coulin with Loch Clair. In the slow-moving deep-brown burn, broad-leaved pondweed grows and foxgloves, wood sage, golden rod and hard fern line the banks. White water lilies and water lobelia flower in the shallows. Further on, buckbean thrives among the reeds at the head of Loch Coulin.

Take the signposted footpath where the track divides and follow it as it climbs higher above the loch, its sides edged with yellow rattle, alpine willow herb, meadow sweet, pink eyebright and self heal. More water lilies, with petals curving delicately, float on the placid water. A stonechat in resplendent plumage scolds from the top of a bracken frond. Birch and rowan grow sparsely on the slopes down to the water's edge.

Pass through a gate that gives access to open moorland, with conifer trees stretching into the distance on the left. Look among the moorland grass for sneezewort, spearwort, orchis, lousewort and bog asphodel.

Use the duck boarding to cross a very wet area of peat to a gate that gives entry to drier pastures close to the loch. Here a black-throated diver busily seeks food and a sandpiper flies along the shoreline followed by its mate.

Keep on to the end of the loch. To the right are spectacular views of Beinn Liath Mhór. The path becomes indistinct but continues over the moorland pasture until a wide reinforced track is reached. Turn right and follow this to the bridge over the River Coulin. Beyond, walk along the track through pastures where a bull grazes peacefully surrounded by many cows and calves. Walk past the farm buildings and continue along the track as it bears to the right. This circles around the other side of Loch Coulin, passing through Scots pine and rhododendrons.

Further along, a clump of birch hosts a pair of tree creepers, several coal tits and a family of goldcrests. A wren tries to collect her large brood, some youngsters having strayed too far. What a joy it is to hear so much birdsong after the quietness of the plantation on the other side.

In the loch, large fish leap from the water after a myriad of hovering gnats. High on the slopes of the Coulin Forest red deer graze, the antlers of the stags clearly outlined against the blue sky. Further on along the path a large knoll, covered with heather and silver birch, stretches out into the loch. Here more stonechats flit about the wire deer fence around the small peninsula.

Continue along the track, keeping to the left fork where it divides. Follow it as it passes through dense, very tall rhododendrons. Cross the bridge over the river between the two lochs and then return along the metalled road taken at the beginning of the walk.

5 $^1/_2$ miles
4 hours

9. Inveralligin to Diabaig

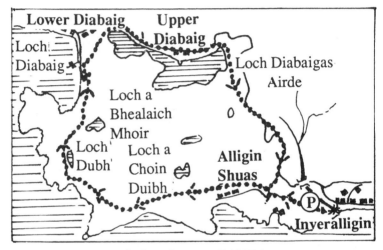

O.S. reference 841574

Park opposite the phone box on the edge of the village of Inveralligin. Turn right and walk along the reinforced road to the bridge over the Abhainn Alligin. Beyond, continue in front of the cottages. Here, a painted white sign points the way to Diabaig. The path runs up the slope by the fence of the last cottage, passing beneath beech and oak. Look for the red causeway that ascends the side of the sandstone cliff and then follow the distinct path that crosses the moorland above. Milkwort and lousewort grow here and meadow pipits flit from rock to rock, trilling plaintively.

To the right, Beinn Alligin is wreathed in dense cloud and Beinn Dearg and Liathach are swathed in veils of mist. A good path crosses between heather, pungent bog myrtle, eyebright, butterwort and small silver birches. Where it comes to the edge of a very narrow road, walk on ahead. From the birches that shadow the way come the curring calls of mistle thrushes. Large pink blossoms cover rose bushes and a wren scolds from deep in their foliage.

At the division of the road, take the left fork and walk through the hamlet of Alligin Shuas. Continue on to a track through the woods where the road ends. Look for a male siskin sitting on an electricity cable. Beyond the trees lies a small beach just made for summer swims. Here a sandpiper flies low over the water to rocks across the bay.

Walk along the path, with hazel and rowan to the right, until you reach a pale-green gate with painted directions for Diabaig. The way continues through the wood, where bracken grows densely beneath birch, the roots of which are crag-fast between the sandstone boulders. Toadstools grow about the path where it passes under hazel. To the left, a noisy stream tumbles through the trees.

After climbing steadily through the wood, cross the stream and pass through a gate onto the open moorland. Below lie the islands in Loch Shieldaig and beyond towers Beinn Damh. A dragonfly flits over the heather. The path joins another coming from above Alligin Shuas. From this point on the way is cairned.

The path moves close to the cliff edge, from where there are wonderful views back into Upper Loch Torridon. Follow the distinct path as it passes through a veritable flower garden. It then comes close to the edge of a very steep cliff and here grow all the heathers, beautiful St John's wort, thyme — both common and wild — and the pretty wood sage. And then the cliff edge is left behind and the way lies between huge rocky outcrops. Far away, across Loch Shieldaig, lie the white houses of Shieldaig.

In the next hollow, where bracken grows profusely, a male stonechat gives its alarm call and flits anxiously about the bracken, seeking to draw the walker away from its nest. Its silent mate stays close. Cross the two small streams, where procumbent willow grows, and then over the top of the next hill you can see Port an Lagaidh below.

Walk on through the bog myrtle, which is laden with tiny yellow fruit. Here, sundew grows with tiny white flowers still in bud. Below lies a croft house. Look for the 'path' sign painted clearly on a huge boulder. Juniper grows in crevices among the boulders.

Climb steadily out of the hollow, where tiny rose bushes grow along the path. A few more steps to the top and the lovely Lochan Dubh lies to the right. The delicate lobelia still flowers close to the shore, its rosettes of green leaves spangling the mud. At the far end of the loch spearwort, bright yellow in the sunlight, waves in the gentle breeze. But what catches the eye are the magnificent white water lilies spreading across the water.

The path meanders along the side of the still water. This is the place to picnic. Enjoy the perfect peace of this lovely hollow, which is surrounded by towering outcrops and moorland flowers, and then walk on along the path as it begins to climb. Over the brow of the hill lies Loch a Bhealaich Mhoir, a larger lochan but set in a similar hollow surrounded by high hills. More water lilies grow and about the shore flourishes upright sundew with tall, slender-stalked, white flowers.

Continue climbing, passing between huge rocky outcrops. And then Loch Diabaig lies far below, with its harbour sheltering many small boats. The path begins the descent, clear to follow but full of boulders. Care is required here. The way comes close to the cliff edge and then crosses a rock fall. Below to the left you can see a large fish farm where huge fish jump across their cages and the calls of gulls reverberate against the rocky sides of the hill-girt basin.

Just when you think the path must be down for good it begins to climb steeply once more. it curves round and then the long climb down begins, steeply and relentlessly. In a very few minutes you reach the gate out of the ravine, but do descend with care. Pass through the gate, which is shaded by two large rowans, and follow the white waymarkings that direct you downhill. The lovely path passes beneath rowan, hazel and birch, over wide slabs of sandstone. Two blue footpath signs direct you to the gate to Lower Diabaig.

When you can tear yourself away from the tiny hamlet, return to the footpath sign and walk straight ahead, keeping to the good path that runs close to the tumbling stream. Go past a shed and continue upwards. Beyond the wall, veer to the left and then to the right where the continuation of the path is indistinct. The path, keeping quite close to the noisy burn, ascends through summer vegetation until a gate is reached. Look back often to Diabaig and its harbour far below. Beyond the gate follow the narrow, distinct path. Look over to the pretty waterfall on the left.

To the right lies Loch a' Mhullaich, where a sandpiper calls as it flies. Cross the river on convenient boulders and walk to the road. Turn right. Here look for the snipe feeding in the ooze beside the road. it flies off with a strong, fast flight, a dark bird with long thin wings.

Continue past Upper Diabaig and onto the side of Loch Diabaigas Airde. Just beyond a ruined building on the right lies a gate. This is the start of the footpath that drops down to the side of the loch and then climbs uphill following the line of the telegraph poles. This footpath cuts off a wide tedious loop of the road.

Walk on beside a small lochan and then take another footpath on the left that drops steeply downhill, following the line of poles once again. This path avoids another wide loop in the road. Ahead lies a wonderful panorama of the towering mountains rising upwards around the still waters of Upper Loch Torridon.

At the road junction, follow the signpost directions for Alligin Shuas. Walk down the narrow, deserted road and bear left where it forks. Walk on until the start of the path over the moorland to Inveralligin.

9 $^1/_2$ miles
7 hours

10. Beinn Alligin via Tom na Gruagaich

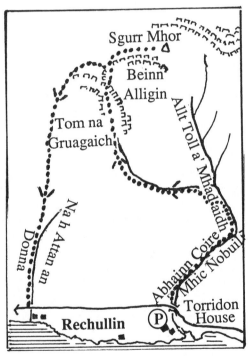

O.S. reference 869577

Park in the car park on the west side of the bridge over Abhainn Coire Mhic Nòbuil between Torridon and the turn-off for Inveralligin. Cross the bridge and walk up the path on the left. It leads through Scots pine beneath which grow willow, bog myrtle, heather and asphodel. A small path to the left leads to the dramatic Eas Rob waterfall.

Beyond the plantation, young silver birches colonise the slopes and from these comes the continual chatter of a mixed flock of tits. A profusion of birch and alder line the banks of the lovely burn and its spectacular tumbling fills the air with sound.

Once the trees are left behind, take the second distinct path left to a railed bridge across the burn. Strike up the path ahead, a joy to climb in a dry summer but very wet after rain. Tormentil and bedstraw grow in abundance and these pretty yellow flowers brighten the way. Towards the entrance of the cove in the face of Tom na Gruagaich, you reach a hurrying beck descending in a series of glorious falls. Mossy saxifrage grows in lush cushions beside the racing water and tiny frogs hop among the plants.

The path continues into the cove and ahead lies a long, steep climb to the col above. Walk on to a small cairn from where there is an excellent view of the golden sands of Gairloch. Out to sea stretches the Isle of Skye with the Cuillin, Storr and Quiraing mountains spiking upwards.

A short climb to the right over sandstone rubble brings you to the cairn on top of Tom na Gruagaich — a good place for a well-earned rest.

Leave the cairn by a path off to the left. Scramble down over huge sandstone boulders on the way to the saddle. Towards the bottom of the descent, a wide terrace of sandstone stretches across the ridge and presents an awkward step. Overcome this by moving to the left. To the right of the path is the deep, sheer-sided Toll a' Mhadaidh.

Beyond the saddle, a grassy path leads upwards. It soon deteriorates into a stony way as it ascends to Sgurr na Tuaigh — a small summit on Beinn Alligin. Walk downhill for a short way, before beginning the steep ascent to the main summit of Beinn Alligin, called Sgurr Mhór. On the way up you pass close to a great cleft, which drops straight down for hundreds of feet

into the cove below. The path comes right to the edge of the great cleft but can be easily avoided by moving away to the left onto rocky slopes covered with lady's mantle and club mosses.

Just over the brow and to the left stands a substantial cairn on the summit (3232 feet) from which there is a magnificent view of the Horns of Alligin, with Beinn Dearg and other spectacular mountain tops of Wester Ross beyond. On a good day the view is splendid and a great reward for the long struggle upwards.

The path continues onwards for those who wish to walk over the Horns, but the walk described here returns past the huge cleft and down the dip just below the lesser summit. Strike down the grassy slopes to below the boulders that cloak the smaller summit. Then bear away to the left over moorland where bog asphodel waves in the breeze and heather and tormentil grow. Here grouse breed and more tiny frogs hop over the damper vegetation.

Continue around the skirts of the mountain — a long, demanding walk, with magnificent views of the loch below and Applecross beyond. Walk on until you reach a fence stretching ahead across the slopes. Follow this for a mile until just before it turns to the right, downhill. Pass through the fence and follow the stream, Na h Altan an Donna, down the mountain slopes. Far below you can see the Diabaig to Torridon road. This is your goal. Keep beside the stream as it passes through a gap in the outcrops. Go through a gate and walk on to the road. This is a rough but safe descent avoiding substantial outcrops on either side.

Turn right and walk towards the car park.

8 miles
8 hours

11. Walk through Coire Dubh Mor to Coire Mhic Fhearchair

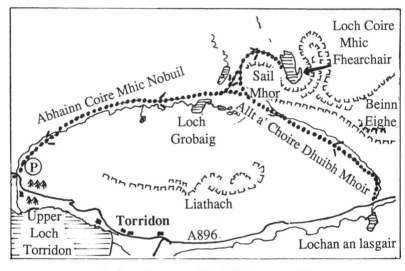

O.S. reference 869577 (car park)
O.S. reference 958569 (start of walk)

Park in the car park at Abhainn Coire Mhic Nòbuil bridge and then wait by the bridge for the ten o'clock post bus. This takes you through Torridon to Annat where the bus turns round and continues through Glen Torridon. The bus sets you down at the car park just before the bridge over the Allt a' Choire Dhuibh Mhóir. The path leaves the road just before the bridge. Look for a dipper feeding in the fast-flowing stream.

The path climbs steadily uphill, passing between the eastern flank of Liathach and the western slopes of Beinn Eighe. The moorland on either side is starred with summer flowers and pipits flit over the heather.

After a long climb upwards, cross the Allt a' Choire Dhuibh Mhóir by two sets of stepping stones. Small lochans close to the path are bordered with cotton grass. Just beyond a slightly larger lochan, by a large cairn, leave the main path and take a cairned path off to the right below Sàil Mhor. As the path climbs, look left to a string of lochans and beyond to a glimpse of Upper Loch Torridon to the west. Continue climbing along the well-defined path.

The path becomes more rocky and the easiest way is to follow the line of cairns. These, eventually, lead you to the right. The path climbs steeply, keeping parallel with splendid sandstone terracing stretching away to the right. Over these terraces tumble three magnificent waterfalls. The highest one drops from the loch above and is caught by the wind, which draws spray high into the air.

Walk uphill over the ridge — the rim of the magnificent Coire Mhic Fhearchair. Beyond lies the secluded little Loch Coire Mhic Fhearchair, where the wind purls the surface of the water. Beyond, rearing upwards is the triple buttress, part of Beinn Eighe. To the right tower the buttresses and screes of Sàil Mhor and to the left the steep rock-strewn sides of Ruadh-stac Mór.

This is the place to picnic. A pair of dippers fly low over the water, one alighting on a small rocky island before running into the lock after prey. A wheatear flies about the rocks but always returns to a small hole under a huge boulder. And then one of those magic moments occurs when a small white bird flies swiftly about the rocks at the edge of the loch. As it flits, the black feathers of its wings and tail accentuate the whiteness of the remainder of its plumage. It is a snow bunting enjoying the thin sunshine.

Leave the coire by the same route taken on entering. Look to the right for tantalising views of Loch Maree and the trees lining the shore. Walk back along the rocky path to where it divides, close to the start of Loch nan Cabar. Take the lower path, where you will find bilberry loaded with lush berries, procumbent juniper, pink orchis, alpine lady's mantle, club mosses and golden rod.

Below the path to the right lie more lochans between Beinn Dearg and Sàil Mhor. Black grouse feed in family groups below the boulders and when disturbed fly a short distance to settle once more. Small frogs hop about among the long moorland grass.

Once the main path is regained, turn right and keep beside the Abhainn Coire Mhic Nòbuil for three miles. The route is distinct and easy to follow, helped by restoration work to the path and the gullying of the beds of small streams where they bisect it. But there are still wet patches to cross and after rain the peat holds a large volume of water.

It is a grand path to walk, with the flaring side of Liathach to the left and Beinn Dearg to the right. Loch Grobaig is covered in reeds and broad-leaved pondweed. Small waterfalls descend noisily. Petrified roots of ancient trees lie exposed where the peat is dry and has contracted.

Turn left at the junction with the path coming from the Bealach a' Chòmhla and continue beside the Allt à Bhealaich. Just beyond the junction of the paths is the confluence of the two rivers, the Allt à Bhealaich and the Abhainn Coire Mhic Nòbuil. Cross the plank bridge and walk on beside the latter. A splendid waterfall tumbles down the far bank, adding its water to the main river. Soon the path passes among birch trees and then through pines to the road. The car park lies opposite. Enjoy the Eas Mor waterfall as you cross the bridge.

12 miles
7 hours

12. Walk along the Shore from Inveralligin to Torridon

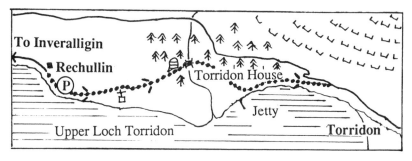

O.S. reference 856576

Drive along through Inveralligin to Rechullin (the end of the road), and park neatly. Look up and you may see one of the pair of golden eagles that nest nearby. The bird soars and sails without flapping its wings and occasionally hovers momentarily, its wings outstretched, its pinions separated and turning upwards. A magnificent sight for the start of the walk.

Stride downhill beneath sycamore, ash and birch past a croft house on the right. Walk along the shore, where a small boat bobs up and down and the smell of the sea refreshes you. As the path begins to climb, there is a splendid view of Upper Loch Torridon. To the left lies Beinn Alligin, its top veiled in mist. Soon the walk continues along the cliffs with bracken, heather and hawkweed lining the verges. Across the water lies Beinn Damh (see Walk 7).

Follow the path, from where you can see oyster-catchers, their piping filling the air. Soon the path swings away from the shore and passes behind the Torridon Church of Scotland. Make a short diversion here to walk round the sturdy building, which sits athwart a grassy bluff overlooking the sea. On the far extremity stands a solid memorial in the shape of a Celtic cross placed there in gratitude to a past benefactor — unfortunately the weather has blurred most of the wording.

Return to the path, which is now a wide cart-track and is lined with bog myrtle. Out to sea, several cormorants fly down the loch. Then the track moves into the forest. Rowans laden with berries lean over the path. Pines stretch up the steep slopes and there is a wonderful smell of resin. Beside the path is a small loch with water lily leaves floating on the shallow water.

Pass through the gate and walk between the dwellings, where lofty sycamores and beeches grow. Goldcrests and blue tits call from the branches, high up. Stride on along the path, leaving Torridon House on your left. Cross the bridge across the fast-flowing, peat-stained river, Abhainn Coire Mhic Nòbuil, that has come down from the hills above. This lovely river is lushly bordered with alders, rowan and rhododendrons.

Where the track forks, take the right branch and pass beneath an avenue of sweet-smelling limes. Now you can see through the trees to the sparkling water, where a pair of herons fly towards the head of the loch calling harshly to each other. Continue past the jetty and onto the now metalled track. It comes right to the edge of the sea. To the left huge sandstone cliffs, which support a wonderful variety of plants, rear upwards.

At the end of the track, the narrow road continues to the village of Torridon. Here a decision has to be made whether to walk into the village before returning along the lovely path or to turn back at the end of the track. Whatever you decide to do, there is a glorious view out to sea.

4 1/2 miles
1 1/2 hours

13. Walk from Kinlochewe to the Heights of Kinlochewe and on

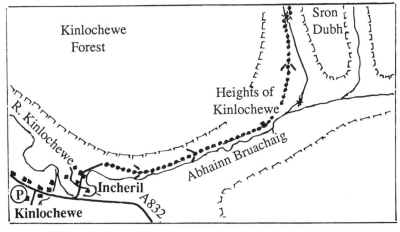

O.S. reference 029619

Use the ample parking in the centre of the village of Kinlochewe. Turn left on leaving the car park and walk uphill for a quarter of a mile. Turn left at the signpost for Incheril, crossing the bridge over the River Bruachaig, and walk straight ahead to the end of the metalled road. Continue along the reinforced track to the deer gate, noting the instructions warning you not to walk on the hilltops during late August to February when the deer are culled.

The wide, flat track moves across open moorland below the slopes of Kinlochewe Forest — a 'forest' that has no trees. Then, after a steady climb over a craggy area, it drops down to the side of the broad, fast-flowing river, which is lined with oak, rowan, hazel and birch. From now on the excellent track continues through the glen, keeping close to the river, which is deeply stained with peat.

High on the slopes, on the far side of the burn, 30 or more red deer graze on bright green grassy areas among the heather. Just beyond them, a white-topped stream tumbles down the steep crags and then passes through a birch-lined ravine.

Stand on the long, wooden footbridge that spans a deep, narrow gorge through which the river roars angrily, its waters piling up in seething foam as it rages against the confining sides. Continue on to stand at the foot of the magnificent waterfall dropping in a wide white swathe of water down the precipitous cliff face.

Below the Heights of Kinlochewe the track divides. Here you may walk on to the right, deep into the heart of the hills. Or you may take the left fork, and then the left-hand path, until you reach the lochs on the tops.

Return by the same route, enjoying the surging burns with their many rapids and falls and with Beinn Eighe, white and awesome, filling the skyline ahead.

6 miles (to the Heights of Kinlochewe return)
2 hours

14. Walk from Incheril to Lochan Fada via Gleann Bianasdail

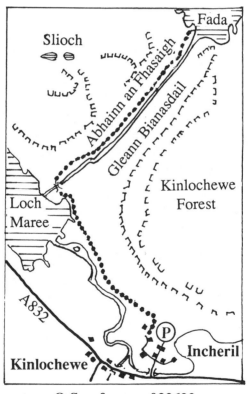

O.S. reference 033622

Drive east along the A832 and take a left turn just beyond Kinlochewe, signposted to Incheril. Cross the River Bruachaig and turn left at the crossroads. Several cars can park just before the gates of the farm at the end of the road. Pass through the gate and walk along a track where sheep graze. Turn left onto a muddy path and walk a short distance to pass through a deer gate. Continue ahead, keeping the deer fence to the left. Enjoy the grand views of Beinn Eighe to the left and odd glimpses of Slioch ahead.

Cross the tumbledown bridge over a burn and walk beside the surging river beneath birch, oak, hazel and alder. Chaffinches call from the trees and overhead flies a buzzard uttering its eerie call. House martins, feasting on a myriad of midges, race low over the water. To the right a fine waterfall drops down the steep slopes of Meallan Ghobhar.

Look for the arrow of stones directing you above the bracken to a drier way across a rather boggy area. Then a wide grassy path leads beside Loch Maree, where a merganser skids into the water on a return trip from the birch above. The path skirts a small inlet of the loch and then continues through a bank of heather before reaching the bridge over the Abhainn an Fhasaigh.

Once on the other side, turn right and follow a narrow, muddy path uphill, keeping close to the birch, alder and Scots pine that line the banks of the river. From now on you continually view many splendid waterfalls, sometimes from the edge of a steep canyon. It is a breathtaking spectacle, but if you dislike heights you can forgo the turbulent beauty of this mountain burn and use a drier path 50 yards to the left.

Continue climbing steadily and follow the path as it comes to the edge of a deep canyon. Look downstream to see the lovely Fhasaigh descending in rapids and cascading beneath birch, rowan and Scots pine, with heather flowering to the water's edge. Downhill too a small patch of Loch Maree is still visible, with Beinn Eighe towering over all.

The good path continues downhill into a wide glen with the slopes of Slioch to the left and Beinn a' Mhùinidh to the right.

Look for the mountain sorrel growing along the banks of the hurrying river. From here a merlin rises from the heather and soars with long narrow dark brown wings to the heights on the other side of the burn.

About the path grow yellow stonecrop, meadow sweet, bog myrtle, golden rod, butterwort, sundew and deep blue scabious. After coming close beside the burn, the path begins to climb steadily and unrelentingly. High above to the left descends a spectacular waterfall. As it falls down and down, crossing the path, you have to stride over it using boulders.

Continue climbing, leaving the burn far below. Eventually this high-level path comes to the top of the ridge and below you can glimpse a corner of Lochan Fada. And now the path begins the long descent to the lochan. Cross another fast-flowing stream just below a magnificent waterfall and descend the cairned path where grouse rise, calling noisily as they are disturbed. At the edge of the lochan, the water — the Fhasaigh — surges over boulders to begin its tumultuous journey through the glen and the gorge to add its waters to Loch Maree. Look at the superb mountain scenery surrounding the lochan before you leave.

This is a long, hard climb through dramatic scenery to the shore of a lonely mountain lochan. Return the same way. Do not miss the path as it turns abruptly left, uphill — there are a number of misleading cairns scattered about.

11 miles
5 hours

Walks 15 and 16

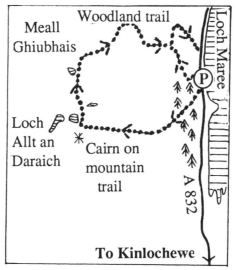

O.S. reference 001650

15. Beinn Eighe National Nature Reserve Woodland Trail

The car park for the woodland trail lies on the side of Loch Maree, on the A832. If coming from Gairloch, be prepared — there is very little warning of the entrance. From the opposite direction, it lies two miles north from Kinlochewe.

The walk begins in the car park, where you can obtain a trail leaflet, and passes under the road. The reinforced path, quite rough in places, is invariably dry! There are 11 marked points of interest, each one detailed in the booklet. At first the path climbs steadily and then steeply to a high point and a conservation cabin — very useful for sheltering when those sudden downpours occur. Beyond from the cabin stands a viewpoint plinth built in the same layers of rock as those found on the side of Loch Maree. From here there is a magnificent view of the majestic Slioch, of the alder woodland of Kinlochewe and the oak woodland of Letterewe.

Heather and bilberry border the path, the latter laden with purple berries. Cowberry, with a good crop of bright red fruit, grows among these two dominants. Towering overhead and stretching to about 1000 feet up the mountain slopes (the natural limit of tree growth) are Scots pine, the trees that once grew in abundance throughout the Highlands. Here in the reserve you will see pines in all stages of growth.

Moths fly across the path and in the damper areas dragonflies hunt their prey. Look for the droppings left on the rocks of the path by a pine marten. Goldcrests and coal tits call from the pines.

The path descends quite steeply for a short distance and then passes into a birch woodland that grows about a stream. Here wrens and robins call and you may see the flash of the red tail of a redstart or hear the drumming of the great spotted woodpecker.

The trail crosses the road and then returns along the shore of Loch Maree, where black-throated divers and red-breasted mergansers swim.

1 ^{1}/$_2$ miles
1 hour

16. Beinn Eighe National Nature Reserve Mountain Trail

Park as for the woodland trail (see Walk 15). The mountain trail starts and finishes at the car park. It is four miles long and takes about four to five hours to complete. For much of the way the trail is steep and rough and walking boots are essential. Take waterproofs, food, and extra clothing such as a woolly hat, gloves and a jumper so that you are prepared for a change in the weather and also for the resultant drop in the temperature as you climb. A trail leaflet can be obtained at the car park.

Walk through the sylvan birch glades beside the hurrying Allt na h-Airdihe where tall heather and some bracken grow. Follow the good path as it begins to ascend through pines and rowan. It then moves out onto an open area with grand views down to Loch Maree and across to the falls on the opposite shore.

Continue along the path as it moves into more pines, where a family of young wrens flit about the undergrowth. Bilberry laden with dark blue berries and cowberry with red fruit grow here, and scattered among the plants are dark pink-topped toadstools. Cross the Alltan Mhic Eoghainn by a stride and look upstream to the magnificent waterfall above.

Beyond the trees the path zig-zags steeply upwards. The going is hard and you have to scramble a little. Look for the well-placed cairns that help you find the safe way for the whole of the trail. An enormous amount of work has been done to the path and rock steps help you over the severe parts, but care is required. On a showery day you can see wonderful rainbows flickering over the loch below. Some are a perfect bow; in others the colours lie in horizontal bands. Black rain above blots out Slioch but the green of the mountain's slopes is still visible beneath.

Beyond the 1000-feet marker post, the climb continues over grey-white quartzite bare of vegetation. You need to scramble and climb. Prostrate juniper, both club mosses, crowberry and various sedges grow in protected crevices. At 1800 feet you reach the summit. Sit out of the wind and have your sandwiches while you count the many high mountain tops around you.

The cairned route from the summit crosses a lunar-like plateau below Meall a' Ghiubhais and comes close beside Loch Allt an Daraich. After rain, small boggy pools form over the flattish ground but the good path is stepped with boulders to help you cross dry-shod. You next pass Lunar Loch. It seems aptly named, though it was really named to commemorate man's first landing on the moon. Floating bur-reed grows on the far side. Scattered sparingly over the quartzite lie red sandstone boulders deposited by receding glaciers 10,000 years ago. On a cairn a wheatear perches.

More well-placed boulders help you cross the An t-Allt, which comes down from the slopes above and adds its waters to the Allt na h-Airidhe. From now on the well-maintained path begins to descend, keeping in sight and sound of the tumultuous burn. There is a good view from the path of the Allt na h-Airidhe Gorge and the spider-thread path along the top of the sheer-sided ravine.

Climb the ladder stile into a small enclosure, which is fenced to keep out grazing deer and thus allows regeneration of natural pines. Look across the gorge to the white-topped An t-Allt cascading for several hundred feet through birch and rowan.

After the second ladder stile out of the enclosure, walk across large sheets of rock criss-crossed with scratches and grooves where glacial sheets moved over them. Again well-placed cairns take you across this rough terrain.

Just into the forest you may find the boulders across a tributary stream under the water. Look for a suitable place to cross dry-shod, or perhaps wade across or paddle over the stepping stones. As you walk through the forest once more, you appreciate the shelter it provides after the exposed high parts of the trail. Look for the delicate autumn lady's tresses orchid growing about the path among the heather and for the sulphur-coloured boletuses.

The path now joins the woodland trail (signposted Glas Letire Trail) just before the conservation cabin. From here, follow the marker posts to the car park.

4 miles
4-5 hours

17. Walk from Redpoint to Craig and back

Drive along the B8056 through Shieldaig, Badachro, Port Henderson, Opinan and South Erradale. Park at Red Point view indicator and roadside rest, where there is room for several cars. Walk out to the stone pedestal set on a rocky outcrop for the indicator — unfortunately the plate naming the mountains has gone. Below to the left the secluded sands of Red Point Bay provide a warm golden glow. Across the waters of the Inner Sound lie the islands of Rona and Raasay, with the island of Skye beyond. From here, too, you can see Skye's Quiraing, Storr and Cuillin mountains and the flat top of Dùn Caan on Raasay.

Walk down the moorland road, where meadow pipits sit on fence posts. Continue beyond the gate, where the way ceases to be metalled. A signpost says that Craig Hostel is five miles away and Diabaig seven. Stride on past Redpoint Farm, where a female dotterel and two young feed quite

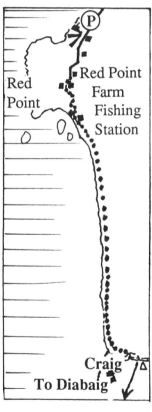

O.S. reference 731694

unworried by the walkers, and pass through two gates. Follow the marks of a tractor's tyres across the daisy-spangled sandy fields, where wheatears still linger. The grassy way is the haunt of pied wagtails. Ahead are wonderful views of Loch Torridon and Applecross.

The indistinct path leads to the fishing station, where huge orange and black nets are strung out to dry. Beyond is another sandy beach. Walk behind the black tin-roofed station and then in front of a deserted house to continue along the path between the shore and the fence. Cross the fence ahead by a stile and walk on along a clear path, through heather and male fern and uphill onto wide sandstone terraces.

The path climbs high up on the cliff, crosses several hurrying streams, and passes through some wet areas, keeping always close to the sea. It is bordered by bog myrtle, heather, tormentil, scabious and bracken. Overhead, gulls circle and shags fly along the coast, keeping close to the waves. Above all circle a pair of eagles, huge black birds against the darkening sky, pausing momentarily in flight as they quarter the slopes for food and then moving on without a single wing beat.

In a hollow just before the Craig River a flock of wild goats graze. These black and white, horned, shaggy animals move quickly away and out of sight as we move along the path close by them.

After four-and-a-half miles, the Craig River is reached. The path moves inland, keeping well above the surging burn. You need to scramble over large boulders as the path moves into the silver birches that line the banks of the peat-stained river. A wooden bridge carries you over the racing water. It is the latest of many, earlier ones having been washed away when the white water of the swollen burn rose higher than the planks. A wet,

indistinct path leads uphill to the youth hostel. Here the warden may invite you for a welcome cup of coffee.

This sturdy croft house was built in 1918 as part of Lloyd Geroge's homes fit for heroes policy. It is now a hostel, with surprisingly good facilities considering how far it is away from a road. Look at the walls inside, lined with cedar, brought over as ballast from Canada on returning ships. Notice the chest in the warden's room; it was floated round from Diabaig on a raft.

Return by the same path. Or you may have a good friend who will pick you up from Diabaig, which lies two wet, rough, rocky miles further on — and with a steepish climb out of the glen. The path is indistinct in places but is marked with cairns, as is the route from Red Point Farm.

10 ¹/₂ miles
5 hours

18. Walk along the 'Old Road' from South Erradale to Three Lochs in the Hills

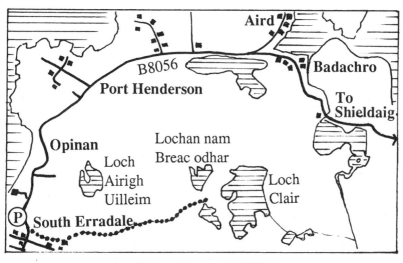

O.S. reference 746716

Drive along the B8056 through Badachro, Port Henderson and Opinan to South Erradale. Choose your parking space carefully so that you do not obstruct other vehicles. By the sheep pens on the right-hand side just before the village nameplate is a good place. Walk down the road and take the first left turn. Look for marsh lousewort growing in the damp areas beside the road.

67

After passing two dwellings, turn left along a wide track between two pastures. The centre of the track can be very wet and the edges a mass of boulders. On either side sheep and cattle graze. In a wet ditch forget-me-nots flower.

At the end of the stony way continue on, bearing slightly to the right along the side of a ruined barn. Cross the small stream behind the barn and look for snipe feeding in the muddy ooze. When disturbed they fly off, ascending into the air with flittering flight, across the moorland.

Beyond the stream take the highest indistinct track, which quickly becomes boulder-strewn. This is the start of the old road that slopes gently uphill. After rain you need to be agile to step from boulder to boulder because the water flows down the slope like a stream. The way becomes slightly easier as the ground levels out and more of the flat stones used for the road remain. Overhead flies a great skua, a brown bird with a dark hooked bill and a white stripe across its primaries, both above and underneath the wings.

Cross the stream on the remains of an old bridge and continue along the stony way. To the left lies Loch Airigh Uilleim, and beyond, the sea. Ahead the golden sands of Gairloch can be seen and behind the village the top of An Groban. Then, where the road turns sharp left and descends into the bog, there is a splendid view over the low ground ahead to the three lochs. The largest, Loch Clàir, lies to the right. To the left is Lochan nam Breac Odhar and nearest to you lies Lochan Dubh. Over the steel-grey water of the lochs arches a rainbow as the sun streams down through the rain.

It is one-and-a-half miles to where the road disappears. Return by the same route, enjoying the good views of Basobheinn, Beinn Dearg and Beinn Alligin to the right and out to Skye across the Minch.

3 miles
1 ¹/₂ hours

19. Walk to Badantionail, Port Henderson

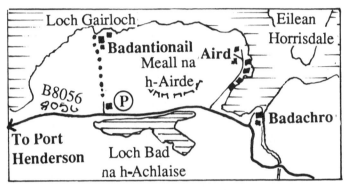

O.S. reference 765738

Drive along the B8056 past Shieldaig and Badachro. Continue beside Loch Bad na h-Achlaise until you are 150 yards from the end of the tranquil sheet of water. Park at the back of a lay-by where a tarmac extension has been created and therefore you are in no way hindering the smooth flow of traffic on this single-track road. Curlews and common gulls fly overhead and on a small green promontory a dozen or more lesser black-backed gulls doze or preen.

Walk on to a cart-track leading to the right. After passing a small dwelling, the way continues out onto heather moorland where meadow pipits abound. Once over the crest of the track, Gairloch and Strath can be seen on the other side of Loch Gairloch.

On the right of the track is a large planting of rowan in plastic sleeves and between these bio-degradable tubes grow small beech trees. The track ceases beyond the enclosure of trees and a wide grassy sward, with some rushes, runs down to the shore. It passes between three small cottages. To the left of the greensward stands a plantation of conifers with a few birch and here a pair of mistle thrushes raise their brood.

From the boulder-strewn beach a couple of hoodies and several curlews rise and fly off. Walk onto the beach and find a flat boulder on which to sit and enjoy the seclusion of this tiny bay. The quietness is broken as a fishing boat goes by, followed by a crowd of noisy gulls. The indented rocky sandstone shoreline stretches away to hidden Badachro. Twenty shags sit on a rock and dry their wings and there is much coming and going of these birds up and down the coastline.

From the beach you can see across Loch Gairloch to the forest in Flowerdale, with An Groban and Sidhean Mór beyond. To the left of the inlet, wide layers of sandstone glow pink in the sunshine and cushions of heather and crowberry hang over the edges. Among the boulders on the upper beach grows English stonecrop and, higher still, a huge clump of flags with skullcap between growing tall as it grows towards the light.

Return the same way. Ahead is a glorious view of the loch, with Slioch topped with mist and many smaller peaks around it.

1 ¹/₂ miles
1 hour (allowing time to enjoy the inlet)

20. Short Walk around the North-west Side of Badachro, Loch Gairloch

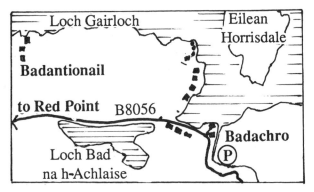

O.S. reference 777737

Park in the village of Badachro and walk along the road in the direction of Red Point. Continue to the crossroads just beyond the dwellings and the start of Loch Bad na h-Achlaise, where a family of mergansers swim. Turn right at the crossroads and walk along a narrow lane where, at the foot of a steep ravine lined with birch, a small stream gurgles merrily. Very soon you move out of the wooded area to where oak and rowan grow sparingly and sheep graze. Away to the right extend delightful views of the village washed by a bright blue sea with the Torridons seeming to lean over it.

Continue walking past some huge rowans laden with berries; in the wet ditches grow flags. From the bracken beyond comes the angry call of a wren. Stride on past a plantation of conifers, the haunt of whispering goldcrests, which scurry along the branches like tiny mice.

Where the lane ceases to be metalled, walk on along the reinforced track. Sit on a boulder beside the path for a while and watch the small boats move in and out of Badachro Bay. Brightly-coloured linnets fly down from nearby conifers and settle on the clumps of heather on rocky outcrops, and a young willow warbler in bright yellow plumage flits through an immature birch. Here, too, a spotted flycatcher makes aerial sorties after insects and then returns to a bare branch of a sycamore — its look-out post. Out to sea gannets dive.

Where the track ends (at two closed gates), turn right and walk along an indistinct path by the fence of a dwelling. Cross the wide sandstone terraces where a stream descends in a pretty waterfall into the sea. Continue beside the fence, which defines the boundary of a garden, and follow it as it turns to the left. Walk on to a large sandstone bluff. Sit here and enjoy the magnificent view of Gairloch and the faint outline of the island of Skye beyond. Here on the rocks grow thrift and crowberry. Look back towards imposing mountain masses, the sun delineating every gully and crevice.

Rock pipits dart from rock to rock along the shore after sand flies that live on the exposed seaweed. Young herring gulls call piteously to be fed from a rock further along the coast.

To return — when you can leave this glorious viewpoint — walk back to the end of the plantation and take the gate on the left, signposted Dry Island Only. The path drops downhill beside a wire fence through bracken and gorse and then continues down railed steps to the beach. It passes below a clump of aspen, with leaves quivering delicately. Turn right and walk along a narrow path littered with bladder wrack and knotted wrack.

To cross the stream passed earlier on the walk, use the sandstone causeway. If the tide makes this impossible, climb the ladder stile over the wall beneath the willows and walk to the small bridge and then to the road.

3 miles
1 hour

21. Walk to Round House on Hills East of Badachro

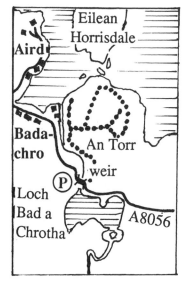

O.S. reference 785731

Drive along the B8056 to Loch Bad a' Chròtha, which lies to the south east of Badachro. Just beyond the weir at the end of the loch the road makes a sharp bend over a bridge. Park before the bridge in a space on the right by a gate, where there is enough room for a couple of cars. There is also parking on the verge by the weir just before the bridge.

Pass through the gate and continue along a good path through rowan, birch, hazel and willow. In a few yards, the path comes to the edge of the ravine through which the Abhainn Bad a' Chròtha surges fast and deep. The path then drops down beside the peat-stained water and continues along the river bank. At the edge of the wood, follow a path to the right as it swings first up a slope and then bears to the left. (There is another path along the river bank but that can become extremely boggy.)

Soon the upper path comes close to more birch woodland. Keep level with the trees until you come to a large clearing among the birch. Here in the middle lie the remains of a round house, an ancient dwelling. (If you have followed the boggy path, you will find it continues through the birch wood to the clearing — the round house lies a few feet to the right of the path.)

Rejoin the path and follow it through the birch wood. To the left, the river flows noisily over its rocky bed. Wrens and willow warblers pass through the trees and the sun's rays slant pleasingly through the soft leaves. Primroses and violets adorn the way in spring and a multitude of colourful fungi grows about the woodland floor in autumn.

The path ends at the beach beside the mouth of the river. Sit on a rock and enjoy the sheltered bay of Badachro. Large fish leap half out of the water, a heron wings slowly, almost ponderously, over the waves and curlews call from along the shore.

Return along the path until you have nearly reached the clearing and then strike up left onto a spur of An Tòrr. Continue along the tops above the birch wood, walking north east. Ramble around until you can find a good viewpoint to see the islands between you and Eilean Horrisdale. On the largest (reached on foot at low tide) is An Dunan, an early fort.

This is a lovely corner of Wester Ross, a place of heather and myrtle, of rocky outcrops covered with moss and lichen, a place to linger awhile.

To return, continue around the high outcrops to the highest — An Tòrr — for splendid views all round, or strike across to the right to reach the clearing to rejoin the path.

2 miles
2 hours

22. Walk from Shieldaig to Fairy Lochs returning via Loch Bràigh Horrisdale

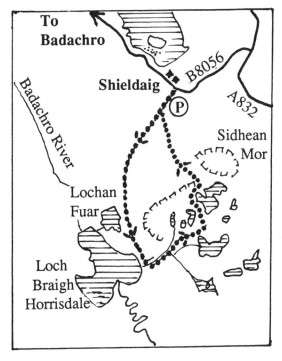

O.S. reference 807726

Take the B8056 to Shieldaig and park in the large quarry just beyond the Shieldaig Lodge Hotel under oak, lime, Scots pine and sycamore. A willow warbler calling softly slips through the leaves and over the top of Flowerdale Forest a buzzard glides. From Loch Shieldaig comes the piping of oyster-catchers. Walk back along the road where willow and flags line a small, fast-flowing stream and pied wagtails chase flies in the warm sunshine. After 100 yards, take the cart-track on the right, crossing the stream by a footbridge. On the left is a farm building and through its open door swallows fly in and out as they feed their brood. Ducks and geese congregate in the yard, together with a horde of house sparrows.

Continue along the track, passing through birch, rowan and oak woodland, the haunt of wrens and robins. Walk on past the sign for the Fairy Lochs and begin the steady climb as the cart-track passes beneath birch with the occasional rowan and willow. A linnet flits across the pastures and tits call from the tree tops. Away to the left small white-topped falls descend under more birch. Large blue and black dragonflies momentarily fly close to the birches and then hover over the small stream that chatters beside the track for much of its climb.

Follow the track as it crosses open moorland, colourful with heather and scabious, pungent with bog myrtle, and with craggy outcrops on either side. Walk beside Lochan Fuar and then Loch Bràigh Horrisdale, a large expanse of water surrounded by smooth, grassy slopes. The track comes to a steeply-sloping wooden bridge crossing a small burn. Turn left on the far side onto the moorland and follow an indistinct path between the burn and the crags to the right. This leads to what appears to be an ancient causeway and avoids some of the marsh beside the stream. From here the path, very wet, crosses left to skirt a small eminence.

Behind the small crag, two very narrow ditches can be crossed by a stride. The narrow path, in some places only a wet muddy way, strikes slightly to the right across a flattish area before climbing a short slope. Ahead the path crosses another wet, flat pasture before ascending a further small incline. At the top of this, the path lies once again across more marshy ground before ascending at the far side to a cairn.

Below lies one of the Fairy Lochs, the path keeping to the eastern side. To the right, on another lochan, a boy fishes for trout from a small boat. Follow the shore round to the poignant wreckage of a USAAF Liberator, which crashed while on its way home at the end of the war in 1945. The plane struck the summit of Slioch before ploughing into the side of the high crags beside the Fairy Lochs. Today a large piece lies on a heather-clad island and another, which looks like the propellor, sticks up out of the water of the lochan. Just beyond grow white water lilies, buckbean and lobelia. A few yards on, to the right of the path, is a memorial brass plate with the names of the youthful crew and passengers set into the rock face of the high crag overlooking the sad scene. Pause awhile with your thoughts in this lovely hollow where the only sound is the sighing of the breeze and the only movement a gentle purling of the water.

Continue along the clear path over a shoulder between two crags and then along the west side of another lochan, crossing the small stream that issues from its far corner. Occasional cairns help you on your way.

Beyond the loch is a small, rusty sign directing the way to the crash site.

From now on the path, distinct but wet and muddy, descends over heather and myrtle moorland. Ahead are good views of Gairloch and Strath. You can see Longa Island at the mouth of Loch Gairloch. It was apparently used by the Vikings for over-wintering. Beyond lies the Island of Skye. Here another signpost directs walkers to the Fairy Lochs.

The path then descends through more glades of birch to the signpost seen almost at the beginning of the walk. Turn right and walk back along the track to the road.

3 1/2 miles
2 hours or more

23. Short Forest Walk to Victoria Falls, Slattadale Forest, Loch Maree

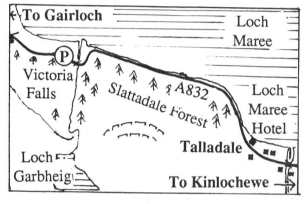

O.S. reference 895711

Slattadale Forest lies ten miles north west of Kinlochewe, on the A832. Leave your car in the car park, which is well-signposted, and follow the waymarks that direct you through the conifers. Wood sorrel and hard fern cover the woodland floor and goldcrests call from the branches above. After a short walk, sit on a well-railed bench seat, overlooking the stupendous falls. A wide curtain of foaming water descends into a seething basin. The burn is then channelled through a narrow ravine and here a boulder diverts part of the flow, which crosses over the main stream. Both fall like tangling ribbons in the wind. Below this drop boils a cauldron of white foam. The water flows on, cascading over ridge after ridge of sandstone into a dark hollow.

Victoria Falls, so named after Queen Victoria's visit in 1877, descends through alders, pines and birch. On the steep sides ferns, mosses and liverworts luxuriate in the continual spray. Continue along the well-marked way, climbing through the trees to a bridge across the top of the falls. From here there is a magical view of the rapids, where sparkling water slides over wide sheets of sandstone before being forced into a narrow channel by a huge bluff of rock. Here the water roars and rages through the confining sandstone walls.

The easy-to-walk, well-maintained path continues through the trees and brings you back to the car park. A wonderful short walk — do not forget your camera.

$^1/_2$ *mile*
$^1/_2$ *hour*

24. Walk through Flowerdale to Loch Airigh a' Phuill

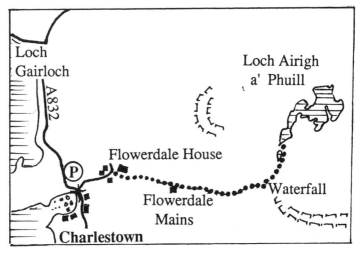

O.S. reference 810754

Leave Gairloch by the A832 and drive south for a mile. Park in the car park on the left immediately before the new bridge at Charlestown. Walk past the old bridge, now restored as an attractive footbridge, and continue along the road marked 'private — except for walkers'. Woodland with beech, oak, rhododendrons and sycamore densely covers the left side of the road and to the right are two man-made lochans where ducks feed and a greater mullien flowers among the reeds fringing the water.

Pass the charming Flowerdale House, with its immaculate sloping lawns, built in the 18th century. Follow the road and walk ahead to the right of an old barn to see a plaque set in the wall. On it is an archer and a lion, together with a Latin inscription and the date 1730. The road continues beneath lofty limes, beech and ash to a gate just beyond buildings named as Flowerdale Mains on the O.S. map.

Go through the kissing-gate at the side of the gate. From here a muddy cart-track continues, passing through an area where timber has been felled. Beyond, the path is bordered by fern-lined banks below trees beneath which boletus fungi grow, close beside a foaming burn. A quarter of a mile further on, the burn is joined on the right by another coming down from the glen above. It passes through silver birch, descending in a magnificent waterfall, Eas Dubh — The Black Falls. The burn falls in a wide white veil of water, dropping 30 feet into a seething basin. If the burn — which has accompanied your walk for much of the way — is in spate, you may not be able to cross but even from a distance the Black Falls are spectacular.

Follow the path as it climbs up beside the white-topped, foaming burn through foxgloves, wild strawberry, milkwort and red clover. Large petrol-blue and black dragonflies flit over the vegetation and demoiselles settle on sunlit rocks. The forest trees stretch away to the left of the path.

A hundred yards above the falls the forest ends. Beyond, the burn topples down the hillside in long white cascades, filling the air with its raging. Beside the stream, bordered with meadow sweet, a narrow path continues upwards. A frog hops among the damp vegetation. Climb up beside the magnificent cascade, which is edged by yellow stonecrop and golden rod, to the rapids above. Higher still lies Loch Airigh a' Phuill and from this issues the burn, docile at first, before it makes its tempestuous descent through Flowerdale.

Before you return by the same path, walk over the moorland, where club moss and juniper grow, to the edge of a large boulder that stands atop the ridge. From here there is a wonderful view over the forest to the loch far below and Skye in the distance.

4 miles
2 hours

25. Walk from near Tollie Farm to Slattadale

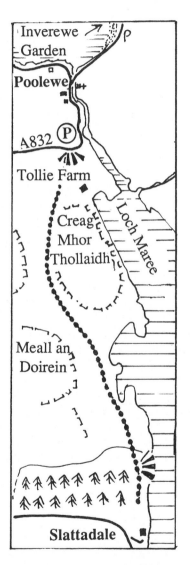

O.S. reference 859790

From Gairloch, drive east along the A832 in the direction of Poolewe for some four miles. There is room for a dozen or more cars on the left-hand side of the road just beyond the well-signposted start of the walk. From the car park, enjoy the magnificent view of Loch Maree stretching away into the depths of the hills. Cross the road and walk back a few yards to where the path drops down a slope. Continue over moorland to the edge of a fast-flowing burn, and cross by well-placed boulders. This can be challenging if the burn is in spate but the rough surface of the sandstone boulders gives your boots good purchase as you step from rock to rock.

Beyond the burn, the path begins to climb between heather and hard fern and then passes below the towering grey crags of

Creag Mhór Thollaidh. It comes to the edge of another racing burn. There are more well-placed flat boulders here, but if these are under water it is better to remain on the west of the stream and continue uphill, walking through pungent bog myrtle, to the waterfall higher up. Here it is easier to cross dry-shod.

Once on the other side, climb the slope to join the good track above. Walk on below the lofty crags and past pretty falls where the burn leaves the lochan. On this tranquil pool of water white lilies and buckbean grow and reeds fringe the edges. A pair of stonechats call from nearby rocks and then flit to the top of a favoured bracken frond. Alpine lady's mantle, asphodel, club moss and Icelandic moss grow about the path. Look back to a glorious view of Loch Ewe and its islands.

Stride on along the path over sandstone eminences where procumbent juniper straggles. Follow it where it passes between two more lochans where more water lilies and buckbean flourish. After climbing several more rises and descending more dips in the path Loch Maree, with its tree-clad islands, lies below. This lovely extensive stretch of water continues into the misty distance, its banks lined with conifers. Slioch, its head in the clouds, towers high over all the other enclosing heights. In the far distance you can see the veiled tops of Beinn Eighe and Beinn Alligin. A small boat moves slowly over the gently lapping water, its occupants fishing.

From the ridge, you might like to make a short excursion to the top of Meall an Doirein. A track leads off to the right and there are splendid views from the summit.

The path now leads downwards, rough, rocky and wet. Towards the bottom of the descent, look for the series of falls where the stream, which has accompanied you all the way downhill, tumbles white-topped over layers and layers of red sandstone. Follow the path as it veers southwards, still descending. To the right, a long white plume of water drops over the edge of a high crag and then falls in noisy cascades, hurrying on its way to join Loch Maree. Cross the streaming water by convenient boulders and following the footsteps of other walkers. Fortunately the muddy patches are surprisingly firm and generally easy to cross.

Stride on along the path over the moorland where heather, bog myrtle and bog asphodel grow. To the left lies a lochan and beyond is Loch Maree. Just before the forest begins cross the stream, which tumbles noisily down the wooded gorge, then pass through the huge kissing-gate in the deer fence. Ahead lies the path through the conifers, wet in places but a pleasure to walk.

After 100 yards, follow the path as it ascends steeply to a clearing above. From here there is a glorious view of the loch, the pine-clad islands and the mountains. The path gradually descends. Goldcrests and coal tits call from the spruce, birch and rowan growing beside the path. Enjoy an unexpected view down a ridge to the loch some distance below. And then the path comes closer to the edge of the loch and you can hear the water lapping the shore. Pass through the deer fence and continue along the path, which is bordered with summer flowers. Pick some of the wild raspberries to quench your thirst.

Use well-placed rocks to cross yet another surging peat-stained stream as it tumbles noisily down the wooded gorge.

The path ends at a large car park and picnic site beside the loch. Here a decision has to be made — whether to return by the same route, making a 12-mile walk, or to find some kindly tourist who will give you a lift back to the start. You could always try thumbing a lift!

6-12 miles
3-6 hours

26. Walk to Fionn Loch from Poolewe

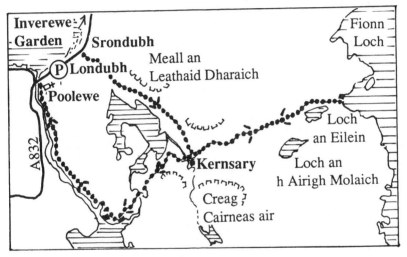

O.S. reference 862814

Travelling south on the A832, pass Inverewe Gardens, with its large car park, then look left for a good parking space on a stretch of the old road between the signpost to Lòndubh and the name post — Poolewe. Walk back on the same side for 100 yards, past Sròndubh, to the footpath sign directing you to the right.

Walk along the reinforced path to a large gate. Pass through and follow the footpath as it crosses a large area of gorse. Beyond the bushes the way continues, steadily rising, over

moorland. As it rises up the slope it becomes cairned. At the top, look ahead to Kernsary Lodge at the far end of the glorious Loch Kernsary. Look back, too, to the houses of Poolewe scattered around the lovely bay.

Follow the clear path down the slope and cross a small stream. The track now rises steadily above the loch, at first very close to the shallow cliff edge, but then rapidly moving away. Step out along the grand path as it passes through silver birch and a heather garden. Blue tits flit from bush to bush. From now on the narrow, but clear, path continues well above the silvered loch, giving good views of its wooded islands and grassy promontories.

At Kernsary, turn left onto a rugged vehicle track. Here begin a steady climb, passing beside a deciduous woodland of oak and willow. Continue climbing, passing through the edge of a conifer plantation, with Scots pine to the left and firs to the right. In the lower branches of the firs, a pair of goldcrests come so close that it is possible to see their bright orange 'crests'. Overhead sails a buzzard, keening as it goes.

The conifer planting is extensive and the track beside it. Among the young trees two red deer watch warily as we pass. At the top of the slope, the trees are left behind and the good track crosses over high moorland, passing Loch na h-Airigh Molaich and Loch an Eilein, before sloping gently down to the boathouse on Fionn Loch. Pause here and enjoy the lovely loch, with its tree-clad islands and its guardian mountains. Ridge after ridge and peak after peak can be seen. Opposite, its grey slopes silvering in the sun, stands Beinn a' Chàigein Mór. To the right, their peaks frequently veiled in soft white mist, lie A' Mhaighdean and Beinn Làir.

Return by the same track to Kernsary Lodge and then continue along the track as it drops down to a bridge over Allt na Creige. Follow it as it swings to the right, keeping Loch Kernsary to the right. At the top of the slope, a snipe takes off, disturbed from feeding in a wet area beside the track. Stride out along the road as it drops down from the open moorland, with the tip of Loch Maree coming into view. Beyond, the track passes through a mixed woodland of firs, rhododendrons, oak and silver birch, part of the gardens of Inveran.

Follow the track as it moves through a large area of silver birch, where willow warblers, thrushes, chaffinches, wrens, robins and blackbirds call. Then the track comes close to the wide, gently-flowing River Ewe. The remainder of the walk is a joy, always in sight of the magnificent river as it flows between wooded banks.

The track is gated just before the church. Beyond, continue to the road. Turn right and walk along the A832 as it follows the curve of the bay. Curlews call, a heron fishes and a herring gull drops a mollusc to break it and then gobbles its contents. The parking area lies half a mile along.

10 miles
5-6 hours

27. A Walk through Inverewe Garden

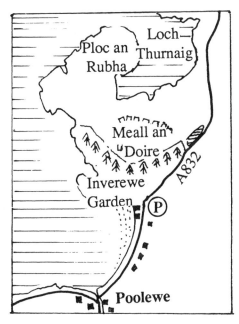

O.S. reference 863819

Leave Gairloch by the A832 and drive the six miles to Poolewe and a further half-mile to the garden. Ample parking is provided and guide dogs only are allowed. There is an entrance fee for adults with reductions for pensioners, students and children. The garden is open from dawn to dusk all year. There is a visitor centre, a National Trust shop and a restaurant, the latter open from midday to 5 p.m.

A guide book with a map showing all the paths is available at the entrance. Many of the paths are waymarked but you may prefer just to wander at will through the paradise of colour, set against a backdrop of Scots pine.

Visit when the rhododendrons and azaleas fill the garden with a blaze of colour. Stroll to the pond, set in a tranquil tree-ringed hollow, its surface covered with water lilies. Wander through the walled kitchen garden that looks over to Poolewe to see the splendid vegetables and fruit and a riotous display of herbaceous flowers growing in the dark brown soil. Walk to Inverewe House and pause on a small eminence to look at Beinn Airigh Charr on the north shore of Loch Maree. Wander down to the jetty along paths shadowed with pines, where goldcrests chatter constantly. Here see a heron fly slowly over the water, disturbing gulls and curlews on a small island. The gulls quickly settle but the curlews fly across the bay calling plaintively.

Follow the paths around the little bay and through dark tunnels where rhododendrons have grown high, meeting overhead. Some paths lead to a high viewpoint where you can look out over the waters of Loch Ewe and see a flock of terns screaming as they dive for fish. Visit the glass houses full of exotic succulents.

How did all this verdant lushness come about? In the 1860s the land to the east of the head of Loch Ewe was treeless moorland. Today, this seems unbelievable. The change from craggy outcrops projecting from acres of acid peat bog and poor upland pasture to the glory of Inverewe Garden was brought about by Osgood Mackenzie. He began to create the garden, confident that the warm currents of water, the North Atlantic Drift, would help him to fulfil his dream by providing the sub-tropical conditions required by rhododendrons, eucalyptus, bamboo, palm and other exotic plants. His vision was realised. His daughter continued with her father's work for many years after his death. Almost 100 years after its creation, she gave the garden to the National Trust for Scotland.

28. Walk to Fionn Loch from Drumchork

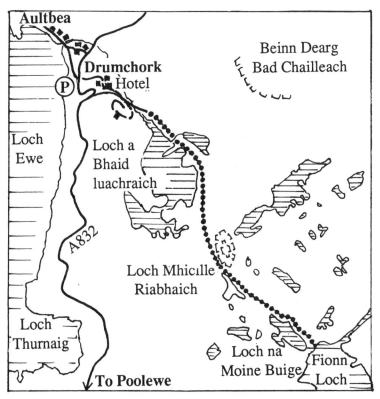

O.S. reference 879885

This is a five-mile walk to a large loch shadowed by high mountains. The track is used by rough-terrain vehicles and is easy to walk. Drive north from Poolewe on the A832 and take the signposted turn-off for Drumchork Hotel opposite the turn for Aultbea. Continue uphill to the hotel and park on the far side of the boundary wall of its parking area.

Walk along the track behind the hotel and pass through a gate. Follow the track, with the naval installation to the right. Pass through another gate and then cross the Allt Beithe by a wooden bridge. Climb uphill and step out over wild and lonely moorland. The track comes close to the extensive Loch a' Bhaid-luachraich, sometimes called the goose loch because of the neck-like narrowing in the middle. The name goose-track has been given to the way because of this. White water lilies grow and birch trees thrive on small islands away from the ever-present sheep. On the far side of the loch is a large conifer planting.

Beyond the next gate, the track climbs steeply and becomes rather rough as it contours Carn Bad na h-Achlaise. It then passes beside the small Loch Mhic'ille Riabhaich — supposedly named after a 16th-century outlaw who lived close by. Meadow pipits call plaintively from the heather shoots and rocky outcrops and mob the writer's dog as it comes too close!

Pass through another gate of sorts and cross the undulating moorland where some outcrops are dark grey and other boulders glow a soft pink when wet. Strike out along the dog track as it continues along the edge of Loch na Mòine Buige, from where comes the soft chatter of divers. Look for the narrow strip of land that separates the loch from Fionn Loch. Walk to the end of the track and ahead lies the large loch stretching into the distance, silvery in the weak sunshine. To the left lies Beinn a' Chàisgein Beag and Beinn a' Chàsgein Mór. Ahead lies Mhaighdean and to the right Beinn Làir and Meall Mhèinnidh.

Return the same way. This is an exhilarating ten-mile walk. Go when the heather is in flower and a multitude of small flowers grow along the edge of the track.

10 miles
4 hours

29. Walk to Loch an Teas from Bualnaluib

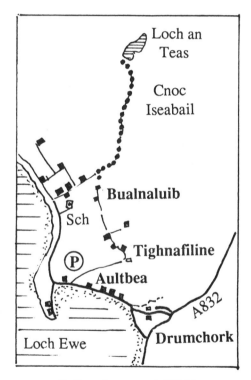

O.S. reference 865900

Leave the A832 at the turn-off for Aultbea. Drive through the village and park on the grassy verge of the seashore at the foot of the turning for Bualnaluib. Walk uphill, away from the sea, following the signpost for the settlement. In August the roadside verges are colourful with bartsia, marsh woundwort, hardheads, large mauve scabious, hawkweed, feverfew and yellow rattle. In the ditches, alongside the road, grow huge clumps of yellow balsam.

Where the road bears to the left, continue ahead, passing through a gate. Beyond, walk up the peat road. This is a good track for most of the way. Where it forks, always take the left branch. The track climbs steadily into the depths of the moor, passing through heather. Here sheep graze and wheatears flit about the rocky outcrops.

After three-quarters of a mile the track comes to the edge of a small loch — Loch an Teas. All around lies the bleak moorland, in great contrast to the lush herbage found in the verges along the roadside. There is much evidence of peat cutting.

Return by the same route, enjoying the view of the glorious bay and of the Isle of Ewe. Beyond lies the Gairloch peninsula. This is a short walk — perhaps for the evening — done only in the dry weather.

2 miles
1 hour

30. A Walk to the Ruined Village of Slaggan and to Slaggan Bay

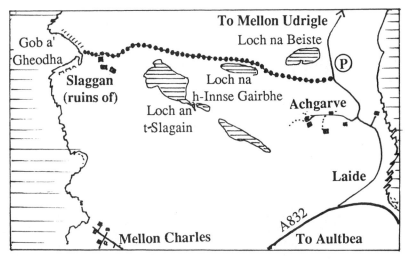

O.S. reference 887941

Leave the A832 at Laide and drive along the narrow road signposted to Mellon Udrigle. Continue past the left turn for Achgarve for a quarter of a mile and park in a lay-by on the right-hand side, just beyond the old road to Slaggan. There is also parking a few yards along the old road on the right.

The road is easy to walk and barely climbs at all. It was once metalled, but is now falling into disrepair. The road leads out onto moorland, with a tree-lined valley to the left, and passes beside Loch na h-Innse Gairbhe, reed-fringed and with a semi-

circle of white water lilies. At the head of the little loch is a large area of willows, over which clamber white and yellow honeysuckle and where stonechats call to their adventurous youngsters.

Continue along the road, which is bordered with heather, tormentil, wood sage, milkwort and daisies. A peat road goes off to the left and in the distance stand peat stacks. In the wet areas beside the road grow cotton grass, bog asphodel and oblong-leaved sundew. Suddenly a red deer hind rises from the ground and bounds off across the moorland.

Follow the road as it passes Loch an t-Slagain, with its two islands both supporting trees. A family of divers call quietly to each other as they consort on the quiet water of this inland loch. To the far left lie the mountains of Torridon. Walk on past boggy moorland with many ancient tree roots exposed; the sight is a reminder of how many trees once flourished in this beautiful part of Scotland.

The road leads on to the top of a small hill, and beyond lies the ruined village of Slaggan and the Minch. Walk down the slope to the gate at the end of the road and wander among the ruins. A female merlin crouches low on the wall of one croft, a dark brown bird with long pointed wings. As it is disturbed it flies low overhead, revealing beautiful, symmetrical patterning. Over a clearing among the ruined crofts grows a large area of silver weed with bright golden five-petalled flowers.

Beyond the gate a grassy track leads to the low cliffs overlooking the glorious sandy bay. Here common gulls and two lesser black-backed gulls sit and snooze. Oyster-catchers pipe as they feed along the water's edge and on the rocks at the edge of the bay shags sit and dry their wings.

Walk on along a thin path, through small blue scabious, to the point called Gob a' Gheodha. Sit here and enjoy the wonderful views across to the sands of Firemore and to the hills north of Gairloch. Clamber over the massive slabs of Torridonian sandstone that litter this impressive coastline.

Return the same way, now with An Teallach and then Beinn Ghobhlach coming into sight.

6 miles
3 hours

31. Walk from Mellon Udrigle to the Bay at Opinan

O.S. reference 891960

Mellon Udrigle looks out to Gruinard Bay and over to an amphitheatre of spectacular mountains. Its glorious, sandy bay curves gracefully, sheltered by red, rocky eminences. It is backed by low sand dunes and in the eastern corner is a plantation of conifers.

Park in the signposted car park just before the end of the single-track road. Notice the interesting bridge that supports the road beyond the car park. The road terminates in front of four cottages and a pleasing green.

Turn right out of the car park and walk to the left along a partly-metalled track. Here a pair of greenfinches call sweetly from a wire fence. Continue along the track, where it soon becomes stony and muddy. It moves out onto open moorland, passing through banks of heather and pale blue scabious. Soon the way becomes grassy, with a raised centre of purple heather. After half a mile it comes to the edge of a rocky cove, with a delightful stretch of pale-gold sand.

To the left lies a burn, which flows into the small bay. Curlews probe the ooze here and fill the air with their haunting calls. Oyster-catchers move restlessly across the water. On rocks to the far side of the cove sit a row of shags, occasionally joined by others. Redshanks call melodiously as they fly swiftly and erratically across the golden sand. But the noise that dominates all others is made by a small colony of Arctic terns visiting a rocky eminence in the middle of the cove. The birds hover with wings vibrating and tail depressed and expanded as they settle momentarily on the ledges of the rock.

Return along the delightful track.

1 ^{1}/$_2$ miles
1 hour

32. Walk to Waterfalls on the Inverianvie River, Gruinard Bay

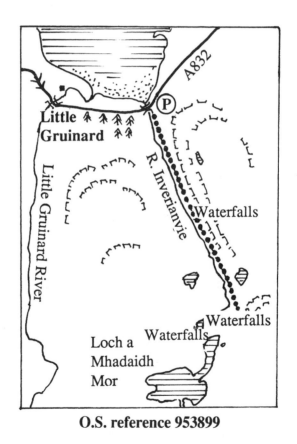

O.S. reference 953899

Drive east along the A832 through Little Gruinard and park in the signposted car park, by the wooden steps to the shore, north-east of the Inverianvie River. Walk along the A832 in a westerly direction, using the sandy, grass verge. Look for greater mulleins, yarrow and burdock growing beyond the fence. The gate, giving access to the path, lies just before the river. The clear path is muddy in places but there are always convenient stones to help you across the worst patches.

On the far bank stands a conifer plantation and to the left of the path grow birches. The way leads through bracken and keeps close to the hurrying peat-stained burn. As the path moves upstream, it passes through heather, bog myrtle, spearwort, and feverfew, and on into a hollow among the rocky hills.

As you ascend, look back to the view of Gruinard Bay. Steep dunes back its glorious sands and sympathetic plantings of conifers soften the craggy hills of the hinterland. Soon the waterfall glimpsed almost from the start of the walk lies before you. The Inverianvie tumbles over the lip in a small fall and then descends in great magnificence like a skirt of lace filling the hollow with spray. It descends through willow, birch and bog myrtle into a deep seething pool. When in spate, the river roars as it races through the gorge and spray is tossed by the wind, tangling with the overhanging trees.

Continue climbing the path to the top of the fall, where a buttress of rock divides the river, before the water reunites to fall as one. Follow the path along the narrow glen. Here the burn races along in a series of rapids and small falls. Where the path divides, take the upper path and climb steadily to the face of the tall cliffs. Here the path follows a narrow ledge high above the river, which, if in spate, surges in great tumult far below. Soon the path ascends a large outcrop and then continues through the upper glen. Walk on along a clear path, which keeps in sight and sound of the now-meandering moorland stream, to the head of the glen where the river tumbles in more spectacular falls.

After the first fall, the next section of the way can be hard going and a little vertiginous. Continue, if wearing walking boots, as far as you feel comfortable.

3 miles
1 ^{1}/$_2$ hours

33. Walk along the Gruinard River to Loch na Sealga

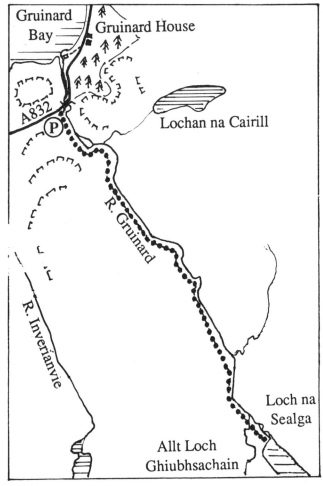

O.S. reference 961911

The track leaves the A832 south of the Gruinard River. Park in one of the several small spaces before or after the retaining wall, south of the bridge over the wide, stately burn. This glorious river, your companion for the whole walk, flows out of Loch na Sealga, an inland loch, your reward at the end of the track.

Leave the road where the track begins, just north of the retaining wall. Here the Gruinard makes a wide swing before descending below the bridge in magnificent foam-topped falls (there is a small railed viewing area south of the bridge). Pass through a gate and continue onwards. Ahead lie marvellous views of dramatic mountain tops.

The track, clear to follow and easy to walk, passes through colourful summer vegetation, typical of Scottish moorland. Enjoy being able to step out, not having to watch where to put your feet. This gives you the opportunity to savour the grand panorama, look at the wild flowers and observe the interesting birds and the fish.

To the left, over Carn na h-Aire, an eagle circles leisurely, without one flap of its great wings. Where the river makes a wide swing, a mile along, a salmon leaps high. Soon the track begins to climb gently, passing birch woodland on the slopes to the right. Then it passes through a small wood of more birch, hazel and rowan. Here wrens scold from the undergrowth and a willow tit and a willow warbler call quietly from the branches.

Continue climbing gently into the glen before dropping down into a moorland hollow, with rocky outcrops on either side and the wonderful mountains ahead. The track comes close to the river, where a pair of dippers busily fish before flying to a hole in the bank. Further along a pair of sandpipers fly along their reach of the river shingle.

In the lowest part of the hollow, the track comes to the side of Allt Loch Ghiubhsachain. Cross on a convenient line of pebbles (it is difficult to keep dry boots when the burn is in spate), and continue along the gently-rising track. Here another pair of dippers feed and another salmon leaps. And then the walker has his first glimpse of Loch na Sealga with An Teallach to the left

and Beinn Dearg Mór and Beinn Dearg Bheag to the right. Walk onto the boulder-strewn beach and enjoy the peace and tranquillity. Look for a diver disappearing regularly to feed as it crosses from one side to the other.

Return the same way.

10 miles
4 ^{1}/$_2$ hours

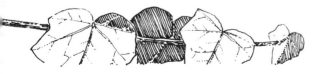

34. Walk to High Ground above Stattic Point, beyond Badluarach

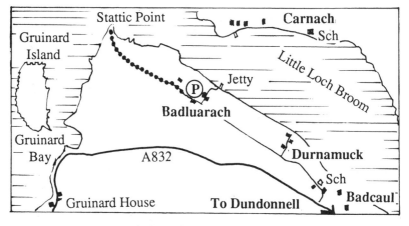

O.S. reference 994946

Leave the A832 at the small road, signposted Badcaul and Badluarach, four-and-a-half miles north west of Dundonnell. Drive along the single-track road overlooking Little Loch Broom. Park in a convenient space, not obstructing any gates, exits or passing places, beyond the right-hand turn to the jetty at Badluarach.

Step out to the end of the road and then continue along the peat track. Spend a little time looking at the peat stacks and the trenches from where the peat has been cut.

Walk on across the tussock grass and heather, where milkwort and tormentil flower, towards the highest point ahead. Though only half a mile, the walking is rough, and after rain, very wet. Grouse rise up and fly off noisily, many meadow pipits call from heather stalks, a common gull careens overhead and several hoodie crows probe in a large wet area.

Clamber over the sandstone and heather to the cairn on the top of the high point above Stattic Point. The magnificent view from here makes the hard, short walk worthwhile. To the left lies Gruinard Island, once contaminated with the anthrax virus. Beyond, the sands of Mellon Udrigle glow golden in the sunlight. Ahead, out to sea, lie the Summer Isles, green and inviting. To the right you can see the lighthouse at Cailleach Head and the path over the hill behind the school at Scoraig. Further to the right lies Coigach, its head in the clouds, over the other side of Loch Broom, which is hidden from view.

Return by the same route, using the peat stacks and the peat road to guide you back to the single-track road.

2 miles
1 ¹/₂ hours

35. Ardessie Falls

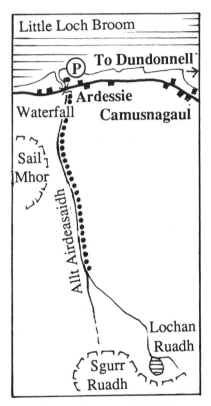

O.S. reference 052897

Dundonnell is the name given to a few scattered houses, a hotel and a petrol station lying along Little Loch Broom. It is over-shadowed by the rugged An Teallach. Further west along the lochshore lies the Ardessie Falls.

Park in a large lay-by, on the left-hand side of the road, two-and-a-half miles from Dundonnell. Walk back along the road on the wide grassy verge, beneath the towering sandstone crags. Look for the colourful floral gardens growing on the ledges beneath birch and rowan.

The Allt Airdeasaidh descends in a tempestuous fall below the road, but from the bridge you can see above an even more spectacular 40-foot fall. It descends in white-topped foam into a deep, surging pool under willow, rowan and heather. A bright, green carpet of moss covers the huge boulders that line the sides of the racing water and over these hurry a pair of grey wagtails. They regularly fly into the air after insects, competing with a dragonfly on the same quest.

Walk a few yards along the road to find an easy way onto the moorland on the left side of the fall. A narrow, indistinct path leads through the heather to a clearer path. It then comes to a huge boulder, beneath an alder, jutting over the raging water, and provides a good viewpoint of the falls.

Look upstream to a pretty fall and above that to a cascade tumbling over more brilliant-green moss-covered rocks. Move on with care over the often muddy path, to see another fall plummeting below a huge sandstone boulder wedged across the top of the hurrying burn.

Continue uphill past the huge boulder and a deep chasm brimful with fast-flowing water. Climb on over the rocks to a magnificent hollow where a huge cascade of water streams over a ledge into a deep peaty pool. To the right of this fall another, narrower one, descends beneath a birch into the same pool. From here the water races pell-mell down the brae.

Walk on up the steep slope beside these twin cascades, and follow the clear rocky path as it comes to the side of an enormously deep, steep-sided gorge. Take care here as the exposed roots of bracken can be very slippery after rain. This magnificent ravine is lined with birch, willow, rowan and Scots pine. The rough path continues into the upper glen. Here the Allt Airdeasaidh, after showing so much petulance, is seen as a

delightful mountain burn. It flows gently through the lonely moorland with many a small fall or cascade, filling the glen with its music. The path, continuing parallel with the burn, is wet in places but it is generally easy to find a dry way. Ahead lies Sgurr Ruadh, filling the head of the glen with its bulk.

Walk on for as far as you like and return by the same route.

2 miles
1 ^{1}/$_2$ hours

36. Walk from Badrallach to Scoraig

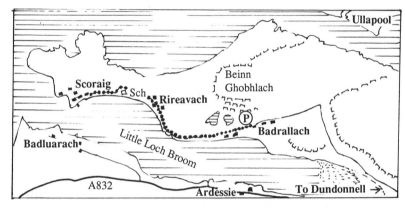

O.S. reference 055919

Drive south from Dundonnell along the A832 for two miles. Take the left turn, signposted Badrallach (eight-and-a-half miles), a single-track road with passing places. The narrow road passes the splendid Dundonnell House and then runs beneath magnificent sweet chestnuts. Just before it makes a sharp right turn, the road is lined with huge limes and then beeches. After passing through the edge of the Lael Forest, it continues onto the open moor. Once beyond the hairpin bend, the road drops steeply down to the scattered houses that make up Badrallach. Drive to the end of the road and park.

The path to Scoraig starts here and climbs gently uphill. It continues over moorland, covered with heather and myrtle, always keeping Little Loch Broom in sight. At times the path climbs high, close to the edge of sheer cliffs. It drops into small hollows in the hillside where bracken and heather compete. Along the edge of the path a small drainage ditch has a profusion of summer flowers; here grow hard fern, butterwort, sundew, cotton grass, bog myrtle, willow, tormentil, eyebright and milkwort.

Far below in a small bay, two grey seals lean back in the water and look up. they use their flippers as if to tread water, and through the clear water you can see their pale underbellies. Close by, a dozen or more shags gather on a rock, some with wings outspread to dry. One or two birds continually take off from the rock and fly across the loch.

After two-and-a-half miles the path, now railed, drops steeply under rowans heavy with berries. High over the towering sandstone cliffs ravens fly and their deep croaks reverberate from the rock face. The path continues over lower moorland slopes where stonechats and meadow pipits flit between bracken fronds and rocky outcrops. On the shore curlews probe and then fly towards the Minch, calling as they go. Look up right to the dramatic cascades, descending elegantly over sandstone terraces. Along the edge of the path grow primrose and violet leaves, the latter plant bearing three-sided seed pods.

Pass through a high gate in a deer fence. To the left is the first dwelling of the village, hidden in a planting of conifers. Nearby is a windmill for producing electricity. After a hundred yards or so the path becomes a wide. sandy track bordered with hay meadows where sneezewort grows. More dwellings are passed, protected by conifers from the gales. As the track begins to climb you can see the houses of Opinan beyond Mellon Udrigle.

At the top of the steady climb you reach the schoolhouse. This was once an old church and has been rebuilt by parents. Continue beyond the school and then take a gate on the left (arrowed in white). This track leads down to the shore and then, keeping close to the sea, leads right to a jetty.

This is an exhilarating five-and-a-half mile walk, along high cliffs and over moorland, always within sight of the sea. The path is sandy, dry and in good condition. It is the only route over land to the village of Scoraig. The other way it can be reached (except by helicopter) is by an infrequent small ferry from Badluarach on the opposite shore of Little Loch Broom to the jetty at the end of the track.

Leave the quietness and seclusion of this remote settlement and return the same way, enjoying the splendid view of An Teallach's imposing mass, Sàil Mhór and Beinn Ghobhlach.

11 miles
4 ^{1}/$_{2}$ hours

37. Walk from near Dundonnell (Corrie Hallie) to Loch na Sealga

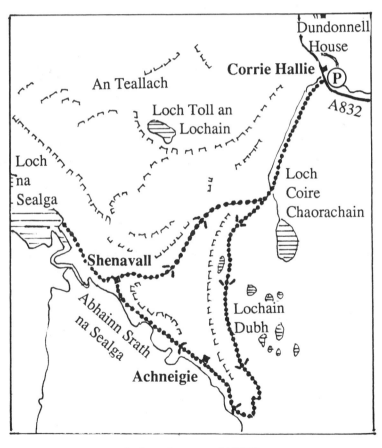

O.S. reference 115853

Park on the A832 in a large lay-by beside the fish-farm shop (Corrie Hallie), two-and-a-half miles south of Dundonnell. Cross the road and climb the metalled track for 20 yards and then walk right to the stile over the fence. Beyond, a track crosses the moor, with An Teallach towering overhead. Pass into the trees that line the banks of the lovely, noisy Allt Gleann Chaorachain. To the left mixed conifers cover steep slopes, part of the Lael Forest.

To the right, extends an enormous sheet of grey rock, sparsely covered with thin moorland vegetation. The track now becomes rougher under foot as it moves into denser woodland of hazel, rowan and the dominant birch, from where coal and blue tits call. Scattered on the far side of the burn are several alders with an immensely thick girth of trunk.

Once beyond the trees, a grand waterfall lies ahead. Before the fall, cross the burn by some 'tank tracks' that some kind person has placed over the deepest part of the hurrying water. From the other side of the burn the clear, rock-strewn track climbs steeply out of the glen into a shallow moorland basin surrounded by jagged-topped mountains. To the left lies Loch Coire Chaorachain with its small tree-clad island. A cairned path goes off right but for this walk continue ahead along the wide clear track.

Stride along it as it begins its long descent into Strath na Sealga, mightily overshadowed by Beinn a' Chlaidheimh. The track descends sharply, crossing small streams that hurry to drop down steep tree-lined ravines to the right. Eventually, the track swings to the right as it comes close to Abhainn Srath na Sealga. It passes evidence of some sort of enclosure or building before passing through a large area of alders.

The track leads to Achneigie, built as two dwelling houses but now used by climbers. Behind the building lies a delightful waterfall. The track ceases at the dwelling but the way continues along a narrow, clear path beside the meanders of the river as it passes through this mountain-girt valley. Look for the ancient tree roots in the peat of the river bank exposed by the hurrying water. Soon the lovely inland loch, Loch na Sealga, lies ahead.

Follow the path and take the right turn to Shenavall, another dwelling used by climbers. Two rowans stand by the house and cattle graze on pastures close to the loch. Stand here and look at the dramatic mountains that attract the Munro baggers. To the south lie Beinn Dearg Bheag and Beinn Dearg Mór and to the north An Teallach. More ruined enclosures lie nearby.

Follow the path from behind Shenavall and continue along it as it climbs steeply. It passes beside the tumbling stream that hurries in front of the dwelling. Here grey wagtails flit about the rocks. From now on the path climbs steadily onto the open moor, where grouse feed, over the shoulder of Sàil Liath. The two-and-a-half miles from Shenavall to the cairns on the track are very rough and boggy in places. At times you pass over sheets of red sandstone. This is the hardest part of the walk. The path rejoins the track where the cairns were passed earlier. Turn left and walk back to the car.

11 miles
5-6 hours

38. The Falls of Measach in the Corrieshalloch Gorge, Lael Forest Trail and Forest Garden, and Walk along Strath More

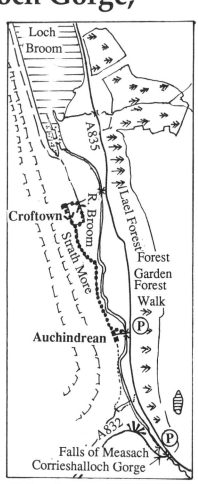

The Lael Forest lies on the east side of the valley of the River Broom. Visit the Falls of Measach first. Start from the car park half a mile north of the junction of the A832 and the A835 (Braemore Junction). Cross the road and walk down the slope to the signpost pointing to the viewing platform. Stand safely, and with camera in hand, for a magnificent view of the Measach Falls in the Corrieshalloch Gorge.

The near-vertical sides of the ravine are richly clad with rhododendrons, pines,

O.S. reference 203783 (Falls)
O.S. reference 196805 (Forest Walk)

silver birch, rowan, aspen, wych elm, bird cherry, heather and golden rod. Ferns dominate narrow ledges. The high humidity and the low-light intensity at the base of the sheer sides encourage a rich flora of mosses and liverworts.

The river, the Abhainn Droma, tumbles gently at first and then drops in a series of steps for nearly 150 feet — a long silvery, foaming torrent. Over the top of the huge falls lies the suspension bridge.

Return to the signpost and walk on through tall aromatic pines to the bridge, which gives you a dizzying view of the Measach Falls. This spectacular piece of engineering was built by Sir John Fowler, the joint designer of the Forth railway bridge. Most of the Corrieshalloch Gorge (nearly a mile in length) was formed some 10,000 years ago at the end of the last Ice Age when torrents of melt water from the ice flowed down the valley towards Loch Broom, as the last Highland ice sheet dwindled away. The present river, lying a vertiginous 200 feet below, is a misfit in its over-sized gorge.

Walk back to the car park and drive on to the parking and picnic area opposite the bridge to Auchindrean (one-and-a-half miles). Follow the sign for the Forest Walk, passing through a high deer gate. Keep right, in the direction indicated by the white waymark, enjoying the view ahead of the magnificent tops in Fannich Forest. In summer the path is bordered with colourful flowers and a good crop of raspberries. Look across to the attractive dwellings at Auchindrean and to the river racing over its pebbly bed.

Pass through a gate into a parking area (Fasnagrianach), and along a ride for 20 yards. Turn left, follow the waymark and walk along a wide forest track. Continue ahead, avoiding the right branch, and enjoy eyebright, stitchwort, ragwort, self heal and deep blue milkwort growing along the verges and the lovely view ahead of Loch Broom with bluish hills around.

The track now crosses a very deep narrow ravine by a wooden bridge. At a crossroad of paths and track, continue ahead, following the sign for 'long walk' and ignoring both the

left and right turns. Further on the sign on the right points to 'viewpoint' and the path begins a steady ascent to a cedar wood hut, with good views across the river valley to the tree-lined gorges opposite.

Step out uphill along a ride, passing through a variety of conifers. Eventually the top is attained and the ride begins to descend to a bridge over the burn, which still hurries through its steep-sided deep gorge. Beyond continues a narrow path, first passing through an area of bilberry and then entering the trees once more. This is a joy to walk, deep in needles and with conifers crowding in on either side. Where the path crosses a small bridge over a tiny burn onto the forest ride, turn right.

The ride curves steadily downhill, its verges lined with a glorious array of wild flowers. Look for white milkwort and the pale lilac heath speedwell. A buzzard glides overhead, a house martin darts through the ride after flies and a dragonfly catches an insect. At the crossroads of paths, walk straight ahead, downhill, to return to the car park.

To visit the arboretum, leave the car park by the gate labelled 'forest garden'. From here, wander along the easy-to-walk paths through the 17 acres of interesting and ornamental trees of foreign and native origin. Most of the trees are clearly labelled. Marvel at the height and girth of the redwoods, at the gracefulness of the cedars and at the soft colourings of the silver firs and the whitebeams.

In this quiet corner of sylvan glory, there is an abundance of birds to be seen. Goldcrests and coal tits call from all sides. Tree creepers assiduously hunt for prey in the crevices of pine and birch. A flock of young long-tailed tits race through the tree tops chattering as they go. Close to the exit gate, a pair of young spotted flycatchers perch on the edge of their nest and call continuously to be fed. The hard-working parents return regularly to feed their youngsters.

The mild climate and the fertile soils enable this splendid forest garden to thrive.

For another walk in this area, cross the road from the car park and walk across the wooden bridge over the River Broom. Continue across the flat fertile valley to Auchindrean. Turn right beyond a gate between some outbuildings. From here, walk on along the narrow lane as it passes pastures full of sheep and then below a large area of Scots pine. A family of grey wagtails flit from the trees to the wire fencing above the drystone wall. They are quite unconcerned by a buzzard flying low through the branches before rising above the trees and circling on the thermals.

Notice the cobblestones under the small bridges that carry the lane over hurrying streams. The lane continues through Strath More beneath alder, hazel, birch and rowan before entering a more open area, with several stately ash trees growing over the wall. It passes a small wood of beech, the trees loaded with mast, before continuing beneath an avenue of fine ash, with a field of root crops beyond.

Follow the road as it turns right and walk on through outbuildings and then past Inverbroom Lodge. At the crossroads, turn left and walk to Croftown. Turn left here and walk back to Auchindrean by the same route.

This pleasing walk, along a quiet lane, passing beneath many deciduous trees, makes a delightful change from the massive plantings of conifers found in the Lael Forest.

The Measach Falls — a few yards from the road
The Forest Walk — 2 miles
The Forest Garden — $^1/_2$ mile
Strath More — 5 miles
As much time as you can spare

39. A Walk through Leckmelm Garden

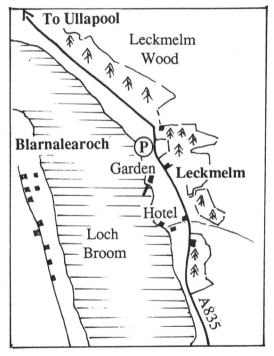

To Ullapool

Leckmelm
Wood

Blarnalearoch

P

Garden

Leckmelm

Hotel

Loch
Broom

A835

O.S. reference 165906

You will find Leckmelm Garden three miles south east of
Ullapool on the A835. A lay-by close by is recommended for
those wishing to visit the ten-acre arboretum. It is found on the

same side of the road as the gardens and lies 50 yards before the entrance, if approaching from Ullapool.

Inside, there is a small box for donations and another containing leaflets. Wander through the splendid collection of trees, some rare, some unusual. Enjoy the planes, the eucalyptus, the many conifers and the magnificent weeping beech. Walk beneath huge rhododendrons and then pass through the gate and down to the jetty from where there is a delightful view across Loch Broom.

Continue along the shore walk, through a tunnel of rhododendrons and then dawdle along the grassy way by the loch. Sit on the thoughtfully-placed bench and look towards the head of Loch Broom. Ramble through all the delectable paths beneath the varied and rich foliage.

The garden was laid out in 1870 by a Mr C. Pirie of Aberdeen. They lay unattended for 45 years after the start of the 1939-1945 war. Since 1985 they have been gradually restored by the new owners.

$^1/_2$ *mile*
As much time as you can spare

40. Walk to Rhue Lighthouse

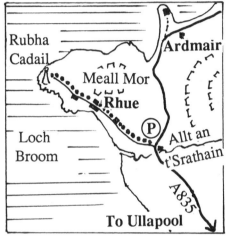

O.S. reference 111969

Leave Ullapool by the A835 and drive north for two-and-a-half miles. Park in the public car park just beyond the signposted turn-off for Rhue. Walk along the narrow road as it passes over moorland with the Allt an t-Srathain racing through its small gorge on the left. Where the road swings to the right, there is a grand view of Loch Broom and of Beinn Ghobhlach across the water. Follow the narrow road as it continues high above the shore, with excellent views across the loch and of the Summer Isles.

At the end of the road, take the narrow footpath (a sheep trod) to the stile. Beyond, walk across the tiny headland through bracken to the foot of the lighthouse. Climb up to the platform

127

for a blustery view. Sit on the huge slabs of red sandstone around the base and watch the common and lesser black-backed gulls snooze on an exposed, seaweed-covered rock. Overhead a buzzard hovers, menacingly, as it peers into the bracken for any small rodent.

Walk back along the narrow road, enjoying the splendid views up to the head of Loch Broom.

$2^{1}/_{2}$ *miles*
As much time as you can spare

41. A Rough Country Walk to Dùn Canna (fort)

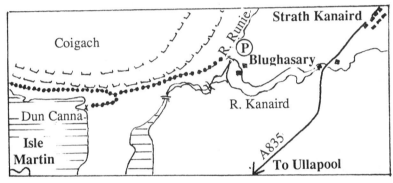

O.S. reference 135015

Leave the A835, north of Ullapool, at a left turn signposted Blughasary. This is a single-track road that comes to a dead end after three-quarters of a mile. Pass through a gate and drive along a very rough track to a car parking area.

Leave by the deer gate and cross a narrow wooden footbridge over the River Runie, where it races through a narrow gorge of sandstone. Beyond, a signpost directs the way to Dùn Canna and Achiltibuie. Walk onto the moorland, following a narrow path through heather, bog asphodel, tormentil and deer grass. The path is waymarked with white posts. It keeps to the right of a deer fence, beyond which lies the River Kanaird. On the other side of the river sheep graze on wide, flat pastures.

To the right of the path rise the steep lower slopes of Ben Mor Coigach. Continue along the path, which is now bordered with bog myrtle, low-growing willow, feverfew, lousewort, and scabious. At the top of the next slope is another signpost directing the hill walker on his way.

Much work has been done on this part of the path and the walker is able to cross very wet parts on sturdy railway sleepers, strategically placed. Just beyond the second stream crossing the path, cairns direct the walker up steep slopes to where the path continues to Achiltibuie. Climb the path and continue onwards if you have made arrangements to be picked up at the other end, or intend to retrace your steps when you have walked as far as you wish.

Just beyond the cairn indicating the hill climb is a gate in the deer fence on the left. Pass through this and onto a track. Turn right and walk along to a gate on the right. Once through, walk first between low-growing bracken and then a mass of sandstone boulders, originally part of a wall, to the site of Dùn Canna.

This delightful peninsula, a magnificent site for a fort, juts out into the sea with curving bays on either side. Wheatears flit about the boulders, English stonecrop grows along the path and a small flock of barnacle geese fly noisily overhead and land on the coastal grass to feed. Kittiwakes fly easily and gracefully over the water, with an occasional dive after surface-swimming fish. To the left lies Isle Martin, with the remains of the chapel of St Martin.

Return the same way.

4 miles
2 hours

42. Stac Pollaidh

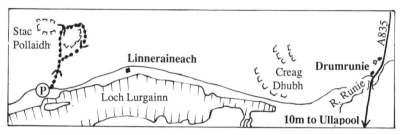

O.S. reference 108096

The distinctive and bizarre shape of Stac Pollaidh makes it instantly recognisable. The short climb to the ridge of this extremely steep-sided hill is exhilarating and challenging, only to be attempted if you are fit.

Leave Ullapool by the A835 and drive north for ten miles. Just before Drumrunie, turn left for Achiltibuie. The car park is five miles along this single-track road, on the shore of Loch Lurgainn. Cross the road to the start of the path that begins the long climb.

At first the path is alternately rocky and boggy, passing through typical moorland vegetation to a small plateau. From here, there is a grand view of the Outer Hebrides. Then another steep, hard climb follows over more peaty ground. The way is stepped by previous climbers and this helps, but the erosion does make it slippery in places. This middle section ends in another narrower plateau and gives you time for a breather and a chance to enjoy the view of magnificent Coigach and the many lochans around its skirt.

131

From now onwards the way is very steep and occasionally treacherous. It takes time, much energy and nerve but eventually the ridge is reached. It lies between two huge rocky, outlandish turrets. An unexpected and breathtaking view awaits. Below lies a glorious patchwork of lochs. It is as if you are viewing a relief map. Beyond lie the tops of Quinag, Canisp, Suilven and Cul Mór.

To descend, follow the rough, very steep zig-zagging path to the west. Then continue downwards to pick up the lower of two paths leading away to the right. Walk this cairned path as it passes round the east end of the hill. Again take the lower of two paths to begin the final descent to the car park after a very satisfying scramble.

1 ^{1}/$_2$ miles
2 hours

43. Walk to Loch an Doire Dhuibh from Loch Lurgainn

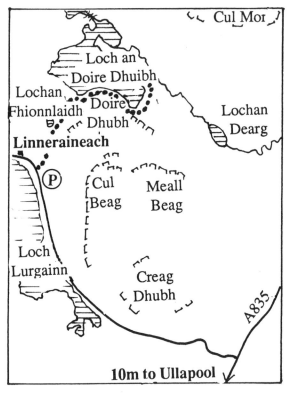

O.S. reference 127089

Loch an Doire Dhuibh lies between Stac Pollaidh, Cùl Beag and Cul Mór. To reach this lovely loch, set in a gloriously peaceful hollow amid such giants, leave Ullapool as for the journey to

Stac Pollaidh (see Walk 42). A verge, wide enough for two cars, well away from any passing place, lies four miles along the road to Achiltibuie. The path leads from the verge and the start is clearly cairned.

The path passes a small area of Scots pine and then continues to climb gently through heather, scabious, tormentil and bog myrtle. Walk through a sheltering fold in the moor to a ridge. Below, to the left, lies Lochan Fhionnlaidh.

Follow the path as it continues over the extensive moorland between Stac Pollaidh and Cùl Beag. More and more stretches of blue water come into sight — inlets, coves and bays of Loch Sionascaig.

Walk on along the path as it slopes gently downwards into ancient birch woodland. Cul Mór seems very close and Caisteal Liath on Suilven can also be seen to the left.

Beyond the trees, the path passes across open pasture below the steep slopes of Cùl Beag. Follow it as it swings round to the left and down to a lovely sandy beach on Loch an Doire Dhuibh. Sit on the golden shore, where the water laps gently, and enjoy the glorious solitude.

Return the same way with grand views of Coigach ahead of you as you drop downhill to the road.

4 miles
2 hours

44. A Walk from Reiff

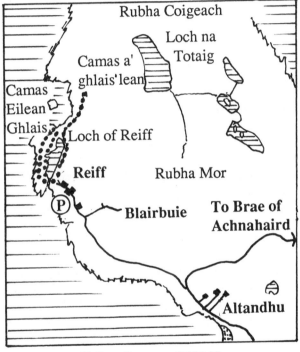

O.S. reference 965145

Reiff lies 25 miles north of Ullapool. Take the A835, then turn left at Drumrunie into a narrow road, with passing places, that runs beside glorious lochs, some tree-lined, and others set in lonely moorland. From the road you can see the sea-girt rocky shore to the north. The many glorious Summer Isles appear to lie at your feet when you descend from the Brae of Achnahaird towards Reiff.

Park on a wide grassy verge, on the left-hand side, at the end of the road. A young cuckoo crouches at the top of a wall, waiting to be fed by its foster parent. A snipe probes in a muddy patch by a pool close by. Walk on and cross the bridge over the exit stream from Loch of Reiff. Once, before the bridge was erected, tiny boats pulled into Reiff Bay and passed between the small harbour walls to tie up in a sheltered corner of the loch.

Once across the bridge, step out over the close-cropped turf. Watch the white-topped waves break on the huge sandstone slabs and rocky cliffs. Look for the pretty sea pink growing in the many crevices and roseroot thriving on the ledges of an extremely deep canyon in the cliffs. Walk on and look down on Camas Eilean Ghlais, where fulmars, black-backed gulls and black guillemots circle the very green grass growing on the top of the craggy island. Several shags and a large cormorant settle on the rocks at the foot of the crag.

Stroll around this grassy area and then return to the bridge. Cross and walk back to where you have parked the car. From here, turn left and walk along an indistinct track to an equally indistinct footpath (marked clearly on the O.S. map) running along the side of Loch of Reiff. Look for the red-breasted merganser shepherding her small ducklings, with their wings barred with white, across the loch.

Continue beyond the loch to reach the sandy bay of Camas a'glais'lean. Here a great skua harries the gulls, picking out a victim to make it disgorge its half-digested meal. Here, too, a stoat runs along the top of the cobbles at the head of the beach, it too after a meal.

2 miles
2 hours

45. Knockan Cliff Nature Trail and Geological Trail, Inverpolly National Nature Reserve

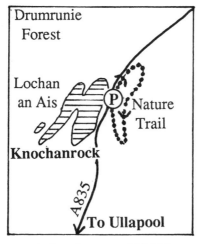

O.S. reference 190093

The Visitor Centre for the Inverpolly Reserve, open from mid-May to mid-September, lies 12 miles north of Ullapool on the A835. There is a good car park, toilet facilities, an excellent wildlife and geological display, leaflets and an extremely helpful warden. Both the nature trail and the geological trail follow the same route. The points of interest on the former are labelled with letters and for the latter numbers are used.

The trail ascends Knockan Cliff in a steep, winding path. At the top, the path over the high peat moor has been covered with raised wooden platforms. This is to prevent visitors' feet breaking up the surface vegetation and allowing the peat to be eroded. The platforms give a safe way of crossing the high moorland. A good path leads down the steep slopes to the car park.

The trail is one-and-a-half miles long and from it you can enjoy magnificent views of Canisp, Suilven, Cul Mór, Stac Polly and Cùl Beag. Far below you can count at least ten lochs visible at the same time, with many lochans scattered over the lonely moorland.

This is an exciting walk. Good footwear should be worn. Some of the paths require some scrambling and care should be exercised. If the winds are too strong over the top of the cliff, be prepared to turn back.

The nature reserve is a vast area of wild country north of the branch road to Achiltibuie. It stretches from the seashore to the mountain top and is home to many rare animals and birds.

1 ¹/₂ miles
1 hour

Other books by Mary Welsh available from the Westmorland
Gazette: